The
WINDOW

A complete guide to
window dressing inside and out *Book*

The WINDOW Book

A complete guide to
window dressing inside and out

Vinny Lee

a Salamander book

Published by Salamander Books Limited
LONDON

A SALAMANDER BOOK

Published by Salamander Books Limited
129-137 York Way
London N7 9LG
United Kingdom

9 8 7 6 5 4 3 2 1

Distributed by Random House Value Publishing, Inc.
40 Engelhard Avenue, Avenel, New Jersey 07001

A CIP catalog record for this book is available from the Library of Congress

ISBN 0-517-15957-0

Printed in China

CREDITS

Managing Editor: Anne McDowall
Design: Town Group Consultancy Ltd.
Projects designed and made by: Emma Hardy
Project photography by: Sue Atkinson, ARC Studios
Color reproduction: Pixel Tech Prepress Ltd., Singapore

ACKNOWLEDGMENTS

The author and publisher would like to thank the following for their help in the preparation of this book:

Anne French (343 King's Road, London SW3), for lace used for the stencilled window on pages 24-25; **Hunter Douglas Window Fashions** for Sunway blind used on pages 78-79 and for transparencies; **IKEA** (25 North Circular Road, London NW10), for the loan of props for project pages and for transparencies; **Osborne and Little** (304-308 King's Road, London SW3), for checked fabric by Nina Cambell used for extending small curtains on pages 96-97; **Sanderson** (112-120 Brompton Road, London SW3), for fabric used for the cascade blind on pages 74-75 and for transparencies; **Joanna Wood** (48a Pimlico Road, London SW1), for fabric used for the internal fabric shutters on pages 96-97.

The following companies and PR agencies also supplied transparencies for the book (see page 128 for details):

Artisan, Byron & Byron, Crowson Fabrics, Firifiss, Lara Grylls PR, Hill & Knowles, House of Shutters, Pilkington Glass Ltd., Pret à Vivre, The Shutter Shop, The Velux Company Ltd.

Contents

Introduction 6

CHAPTER 1: TAKING A VIEW 11
Window Styles 12
Types of Glass 20
Stencilled Window 24
Window Shelves 26
Window Catches 28
Window Security 30
Window Seats 32
Window Seat Cushion 34
Choosing Poles and Finials 36
Decorative Clay Finials 40

CHAPTER 2: LOOKING OUT 43
Choosing Materials 44
Curtain Treatments 56
Curtains Headings 64
Blinds 68
Cascade Blind 74
Fancy Edge for a Roller Blind 78
Bead Blind 82
Simple Drapes and Screens 84
Second-hand Curtains 88
Extending Small Curtains 92
Internal Shutters 94
Fabric Shutters 96
Pelmets 98
Decorated Wooden Pelmet 100
Braids, Tassels and Tie-backs 104

CHAPTER 3: LOOKING IN 109
Sills and Surrounds 110
Window Boxes 112
Doweling Window Box 114
Shutters and Awnings 118
Balconies 122

Picture Credits 126
Index 128

Introduction

Awindow has many functions, from practical to decorative. Windows of all shapes and sizes are useful in that they allow light into a room, and in most cases also provide ventilation, but they also embellish a room both indoors and out. The shape and decoration of the window surrounds plays an influential part in how both the inside and the outside of a building will appear, to the inhabitant and to visitors and passersby.

From the outside, windows create a feature in the wall of a house; they can be framed in varnished or colour-

fully painted wood or ornate carved stone surrounds. Inside a room, the window often becomes a focus for decoration, whether a simple cotton blind or a grand brocade drape with pelmets, fringes and tie-backs.

Windows are also the 'eyes' of a house, allowing the onlooker to see into the room inside or out to the garden or view beyond and provide a frame for this view, like a frame to a photograph or painting.

A brief history

The first windows were small holes or slits in walls that were purely functional, allowing the people inside to look out for approaching enemies and to observe their livestock. These apertures were known as 'wind-holes' or 'wind-eyes' and were covered with heavy cloth or animal skin to keep the out the elements.

With the invention of glass – made by fusing sand with soda or potash – the possibilities for the window grew. Early glass was thick, made in small pieces and prone to impurities, but by the late fifteenth century glass was used more widely, although mostly in ecclesiastical buildings, where it was framed in solid, non-opening surrounds. At this time windows started to take on a decorative role with the use of coloured and painted glass, usually with ecclesiastical and heraldic themes.

By the 1700s the casement window – a wooden vertically hinged frame filled with a lattice of lead which supported the small panes of glass – became popular with Tudor house builders. This style was soon overtaken in popularity by the sash window, which was made to slide up and down in the grooves of the frame by means of weights and pulleys, thus enabling the window to open with comparative ease.

The Georgian sash window saw the size of both the window itself and the glass panes increase – Georgian windows typically had six or twelve large panes in a wooden frame. The symmetry and proportions of these larger windows made them suitable for the Palladian architecture of the time, and the long, tall windows allowed lots of light into high-ceilinged rooms. In Britain, these large windows became even more popular after the abolition of the Window Tax in 1851. This tax had levied a duty on windows and had led to many windows being bricked up.

Sash and casement windows have been popular for

over 200 years and can still be seen in buildings all over the world. In modern times the frames may have changed to aluminium or plastic-covered ones that are resistant to rot, shrinkage and draughts, but the basic shape and structure of these traditional styles have altered little.

In the early nineteenth century, the bow or bay window became the Victorians' contribution to window

LEFT: These curtains made in light cotton check fabric and trimmed with a frill in a smaller check emphasise the cottage-like appearance of this small paned window.

ABOVE: A Roman blind in a small but vivid print is finished off with a contrasting but complementary pelmet, which gives the window a more polished appearance. The blind can be adjusted to obscure or reveal the view.

history. These windows protruded beyond the front wall of the house, so providing a wider field of vision and an ideal place to sit on a window seat and gaze at the view.

By 1869 the Victorians had also embraced the revival of Gothic style and during this time arched, church-like windows associated with the original Gothic period became fashionable. Bow and bay windows with Gothic arched frames were not uncommon and stained and ornate etched glass was often used to enhance the look. Around 1880 the Arts and Crafts Movement gained in popularity and small leaded windows became the vogue. After the First World War there was an urgent

need for cheap and quickly made homes and this encouraged the spread of simple steel-framed windows that could easily be mass produced. The introduction of both steel and aluminium frames saw the development of bigger glass windows and with later advancements in technology it became possible to create larger and larger sheets of glass. Architects and designers used these to make walls, rather than small windows, of glass, with sturdy, supportive, metal surrounds. The window grew in both importance and size and these expansive windows, created from the late 1950s and still

widespread today, can be seen in cities throughout the world, from modern apartments and office blocks to municipal buildings.

Fashions and trends

Window shapes have evolved and changed, as has the glass that fills them. As with fashions for building styles, there are trends for windows too. It is not only the construction of the window that is prone to the vagaries of fashion, but also, and more noticeably, it is the way in which they are dressed and decorated that makes the most obvious fashion statement.

Window dressing is an important feature of interior decoration. Glossy magazines dedicate page after page to the subject and books showing how to dress the windows in your home are much sought after. Fashions in interior decoration have seen curtain lengths come and go, up and down. There have been phases that favour long flowing curtains that lie along the floor, while at other times the vogue has been for shorter, more practical curtains that fit neatly above radiators or just below the sills. Developments in manufacturing processes have increased the types of materials available, as well as finishes and designs – from fine man-made fibres to treated paper, the choice is extensive. Whatever the current fashions, however, do try to suit your own taste and the requirements of the size, shape and styles of your windows.

When you are choosing your window dressing, remember that at night, even if the windows of the house are not overlooked, it feels more cosy and secure to draw the curtains or blinds and close out the darkness. Closing the curtains may also help to deaden outside noise and insulate the room, which will help to make it warmer. Window coverings will promote a feeling of privacy and comfort and become an integral part of the whole room's design.

Of course, although curtains and blinds are popular

window dressings, they are not the only options. In many countries shutters and screens are more common, and these can be folded back when not in use so that the full shape and style of the window can be seen.

Attracting attention

A window will naturally draw the eye to it, being a light source and therefore a focal point. If the window is an uninspiring shape, it can be enhanced in a number of ways. For example, you can add to, or even alter the overall shape of a simple narrow frame with wooden beading or ornate picture framing material. If the window is a regular square or oblong shape, the additional frame can follow the original lines of the window or you could build on it and create a more unusual shape, such as a mock Gothic arch or fanlight.

Replacing a dull window with an old or salvaged version may also create a more interesting outlook to a room. Be careful, however, not to mix styles and periods too much, or the room may appear uncoordinated and messy. In a house where the original windows have been replaced with unsympathetic modern frames, restoring the windows to their original style will help give a cohesive appearance to the whole building.

If the window and frame are already an attractive shape, you may want to emphasise or accentuate this by painting the frame in a contrasting shade to the wall, maybe even in a bright, even clashing colour. For a deluxe finish, why not try gilding or gold leafing the window surround?

LEFT: Fashions for window dressings change frequently; here a simple, fine cotton curtain has been updated for a more decorative appearance with the addition of a bobble-braid trim.
RIGHT: This small bay or bow window makes an interesting feature at the front of this cottage. Bay windows are often fitted with a window seat so that the view or outlook can be admired.

CHAPTER 1

In this opening chapter we look at the basics of windows both inside and out. From their structure and shape – covering standard and classic as well as the more unusual – to types of glass. These days glass comes in many forms, from security glass and double glazing to attractive coloured and decorative glass. Each type has its merits and uses, and it is important to select the right one for your window.

Once you have assessed your windows, it is time to think about the myriad fittings and surrounds that form the framework for any window dressing. Catches,

Taking a View

handles, brackets, curtain poles and finials are all important features of a well-dressed window, both functionally and decoratively, and can enhance the whole scheme of a room.

As well as being both useful and decorative, windows can, unfortunately, also provide access for burglars, so security fittings and fixtures are essential. In this chapter, we look at a variety of options for making windows vandal proof . There are also ideas – including a special project for a stencilled window – for obscuring a dull view, but not the light, from a window without having to hang curtains or blinds.

Window Styles

It is worth taking time to study the windows in your home. Knowing a little of the history and period of the windows, as well as the style and type of glass, may help you to narrow down the choice of window dressing styles and types of fabric. For example, if you have old-fashioned windows such as a bow style with leaded light,

the windows may be small, but prone to draughts. In general, such windows are best dressed with traditional lined curtains because the lining and even inter-lining help to keep out the cold air that may circulate through gaps in the frame or glass. Traditional curtains are often made with printed chintz or jacquard fabric.

If, on the other hand, you have modern, double-glazed windows with no draughts, then a light voile curtain or blind may be a more attractive option. Many classic styles of window, such as the sash and casement, suit almost any arrangement of blind or curtain.

Period windows

Most of the window shapes popular today are copies of early designs. For example, casement windows can be dated back to the early 1700s. The plain oblong frames had diamond or lozenge panes and the glass was thick and impure and set in lead or wood surrounds with a hinged vertical opening.

The sash window, thought to have originated in Holland, superseded the casement at the end of the seventeenth century. Typical sash windows contained six, or later four, panes of glass in each half. The lower half was raised, and the upper half lowered by means of a cord and counter-weight concealed in the wooden outer frame. Sash windows suit most classical styles of building, and are still popular today in both Britain and North America.

Throughout the Georgian period the sash window remained popular, but the windows became bigger – both in length and width – and contained up to 12 panes of glass. A feature of Georgian windows are fan-lights – small semi-circular windows set above doors and over sash windows. Internal wooden shutters were common in Georgian times and offered protection against the weather and hooligans as well as obscuring the view from the street into the house.

Georgian and Regency houses featured bow or bay windows – a curved bay projecting beyond the main front wall of the house. Examples of this style can be seen in the prestigious homes in older American settlements such as Boston. The Victorians also liked this style and in the early nineteenth century bow windows became popular again, especially in seaside residences.

FAR LEFT: You can often date a window by the material used to hold the panes of glass. Early panes were supported by stone mullions (vertical stone posts) or lead strips. These were replaced by wood in the 1700s and, more recently, by aluminium and steel.

ABOVE LEFT: This sash window has a pane of bulls-eye or crown glass. Original glass of this type often has a grey or green tinge and may have small air bubbles trapped within the pane.

LEFT: A modern copy of a classical Georgian sash window. This style of window is popular in neo-Georgian developments and contemporary stone-built houses as well as in cottages.

ABOVE: Bay or bow windows were popular in Victorian times, especially in seaside houses where the view was a feature. This bow window has leaded panes and a decorative arch created by the wooden glazing bars.

Odd shapes, such as round windows and gothic arches are used as eye-catching features for both internal and external decoration, but these less conventional designs are more rarely found.

Window styles rarely disappear – they have been recycled and reproduced throughout the centuries, up to the present day. For example, the Arts and Crafts revival in the early 1880s saw a return of the small leaded window. Neo-Tudor and neo-Georgian houses built in the 1920s and 1930s were inspired by the originals but used updated techniques and adaptations.

If you have a home with original old windows – say Georgian or Victorian – it is desirable to keep them as they were designed and built to suit the architecture of the house. It may be tempting to replace old rattly, draft-prone wooden sash windows with easy-maintenance, aluminium- or steel-framed alternatives, but they will not be in keeping with the overall appearance of the building. Sash and casement windows can be copied, and with

modern joinery techniques they can be made to fit snugly and neatly, cutting out the draughts and eliminating the problems of the old ones, while retaining the style.

Contemporary windows

Contemporary window shapes vary enormously, from architect-designed shapes such as triangles and stars to the more common rectangular skylight or angled window used in roof or loft conversions. Improvement in glass quality and advances in technology have made it possible to use much larger panes of glass, so that whole walls of glass, rather than panes or framed windows, are now common. Glass walls are a particular asset in office buildings allowing maximum use of natural daylight, and also in houses with interesting or attractive views.

Developments in opaque and obscure glass have allowed windows to be put in walls where they may not have been placed before. For example, a window of sandblasted glass can be fitted into a wall of a terraced house to allow light onto a stairwell, while preserving the privacy of the inhabitants as well as avoiding overlooking the house next door. Windows like these, being used only as a light source, have no need to open, so a simple fixed frame with a single pane of glass is all that is required.

The style of windows you have should be in keeping with the design and period of your home. And the style of the window and its location will help determine the type of dressing that is appropriate for it.

ABOVE LEFT: This 1930s house has bow-fronted windows both upstairs and down. These windows are likely to be casement windows opening on a vertical hinge. Small horizontally hinged windows, above the main ones, could also be opened.
RIGHT: This dramatic apex window has been built for maximum views. Several glass panels are fixed but others are designed to open. In large-scale windows like this, it is best to use toughened, safety glass, particularly on the upper floors.

Unusual-shaped windows

Rectangular windows are the norm and square ones are reasonably easy to cope with, but when the more unusual Gothic or round windows make an appearance, many prospective decorators sigh at the task of having to provide some sort of curtain or shade for such an unconventional shape. But unusual windows are an additional feature in any room – not only do they look attractive to passersby from the outside, they are also a pleasure to those living behind them. Unusual-shaped windows give you a different outlook on a view and provide an unexpected focus of attention.

Round and arched windows

Round and arched windows appeared as long ago as the thirteenth century. Windows were expensive and could only be afforded by wealthy landowners and the Church. Church windows often echoed the arched shapes of the interior supports of the chapel or church, and the round shape is thought to have symbolised the sun or a halo.

These early windows were often decorated with coloured or painted glass, and the early tradition for using the unusual shape to frame a pictorial glass has continued to this day. During the Victorian Arts and Crafts movement round windows, referred to as roundels, were often used to frame intricate and beautiful pictures of flowers, views or portraits. Many artists, including William Morris, worked in the stained-glass medium and their work can still be found intact.

The arch window saw a return to favour with the mid-eighteenth-century Gothic period of decoration and the nineteenth-century Gothic Revival in the Victorian era. During that time Gothic-shaped windows were used extensively in homes throughout Britain and the northern states of America and the interiors of the houses were decorated in appropriate Gothic style.

Round windows – reminiscent of a ship's porthole –

are a fun addition to a bathroom or a stairwell, where increasing the amount of light is the prime objective, rather than a view. Round windows are often purely decorative, or function merely as a light source, and so do not need to open. Those that are used to provide a source of air have intriguing methods for opening. A central hinge can be used to let the top half of the window fold down, or a central pivot will enable the glass to swing into a horizontal position, allowing a free flow of air to circulate both above and below the central point.

ABOVE LEFT: The graceful shape of this Gothic arch window is echoed in the back of a fine wrought-iron chair. This modern wooden framed window is based on the style of a much earlier design.

LEFT: This triangular fanlight window has been built over French doors that lead out to the garden. A clever curtain treatment emphasises the height and shape of the triangular window.

ABOVE: A round window makes an eye-catching feature in a plain bathroom wall. Here, the porthole-style window focuses light on the bathtub, which is an important feature in the room.

Round windows can be left plain – just a round sheet of glass – or they can be divided into segments with glazing bars. Some divided round windows feature a central circular shape with segments radiating out. An arched or round frame acts like a picture or photo frame and draws your eye to what it encircles. Where possible, and where privacy is not needed, you may choose not to cover the window with curtains but to leave it uncluttered and unadorned to make the most of this special feature.

Other unusual shapes

Triangular windows are often used to bring light into difficult angular spaces such as roof eaves in loft conversions. In many cases these windows are fixed and not designed to open, but those that do are generally hinged along the long base side. Triangular shapes have been added to tall narrow oblong windows to create a fan light; this angular interpretation of the Georgian fan light was popular in the 1970s.

With the increasing popularity of steel window frames, architects were able to design and have made non-standard sizes and shapes of window. The strength and durability of steel also made it possible to use smaller structures and to support larger frames with more

glass. In the 1970s, steel's popularity waned and aluminum took its place, especially in commercial designs, though many architects still prefer to work with steel.

The recessed or dormer window found in attic rooms and cottages is not in itself an unusual shape, but the recess into which the window is built makes the window appear from within to be at a distance. The walls on either side of the window lead back into the room and make the small window at the end a focal point.

If you are fortunate enough to have unusually shaped windows make the most of them, and if you are planning on adding a window to a room, or building an extension, why not take a look at the less conventional shapes that are available.

FAR LEFT: These angled windows create an interesting and useful feature on a plain wall. The combination of sloping and straight windows emphasise the 'hip' or 'barn' shape of the room.
LEFT: This recessed dormer-style window is built into the roof and is a type of window popularly used in loft conversions. The angled window allows light into the room and can be easily opened to supply ventilation.
ABOVE: This narrow slit window provides a display niche for a vase of flowers. The window has been left unadorned apart from a simple lace pelmet, which softens the hard stone surround.

19

Types of Glass

These days there is an amazing array of glass from which to choose, from plain and decorative to safety and specialist glass that will reduce noise levels and filter ultraviolet light. In order to choose the best type of glass for your windows, you may need to seek expert advice, and possibly check on legal requirements too.

In the early days of glazing, glass was thick, like the bottom of an old-fashioned milk bottle. It tended to be flecked with impurities, grey or green in colour, and full of small air bubbles. But it was glass – an expensive and highly prized commodity. This early glass was known as crown or bulls-eye glass, because of the circular swirl in the centre of each small pane.

Today glass can be toughened, or made reflective, to obscure views and provide protection. There are many types of specialist glass from which to choose, each one to suit a different requirement.

Decorative glass

Glass is visually pleasing; it can be stained or coloured to form a picture over the whole window or coloured glass can be confined around the edge of the window as a border. Small squares or shapes of coloured glass can also be mixed with clear glass to form a pattern. You could even create your own painted glass windows using special paint kits (for example, see the stencilled window project on pages 24–25).

Opaque or textured glass is useful in areas of the home where privacy is needed as well as natural light. Hundreds of different types of patterned glass can be found at good glaziers, from floral and paisley designs to contemporary icicle and wave motifs. These designs are usually either etched into the glass with acid, sandblasted, or formed in relief in moulds.

Safety glass

Toughened and laminated types of glass are both important for security as they are more difficult for a thief to break than ordinary glass. These types of glass are therefore useful for ground floor or basement windows, where access may be thought to be easier. Toughened glass is modified by thermal treatment, which gives it strength and resistance to heat, but it still provides light transmission equal to that of ordinary glass. Laminated glass

LEFT: Textured glass comes in a wide spectrum of designs, from those in raised relief to smooth, sandblasted types, and providing varying degrees of obscurity.

ABOVE LEFT: A small internal window has been made into an attractive feature with the imaginative use of diamond-shaped glazing bars and two different types of textured glasses.

ABOVE: Thick glass bricks obscure the view from a basement kitchen but allow natural light to enter into what would otherwise be a dark room.

consists of two or more sheets of ordinary or treated glass bonded together under heat and pressure by interlayers of transparent polymer. This type of safety glass can also help with noise reduction and ultraviolet light protection, reducing fading and discoloration of fabrics by absorbing 99 percent of the ultra-violet radiation.

Another type of glass that offers improved safety and security, as well as reduced glare and heat loss, is film applied glass. The film is a tough sheet of micro-thin high-clarity polyester that can be easily applied in situ to the interior or exterior of existing glass. The film will also help to contain fragments of glass if the window or pane is broken, and if a translucent or opaque film is used it can provide privacy by obscuring the view.

If you have installed safety or toughened glass in your home, do make sure that there is an easily accessible exit route in case of fire. Bolted and locked security windows and toughened glass will make leaving the room through a window a difficult and time-consuming procedure.

As a result of the increasing popularity of large areas of glass, some countries have passed legislation regarding safety requirements and the use of safety glazing in 'critical locations', for example in areas where there are tall, floor to ceiling windows and French doors, or glazing which extends below hip level. Guidelines recommend the use of safety glazing material in any glazed areas that are below 1500mm above finished floor level, in doors, and in side panels within 300mm of either edge of a door. In any case, if you are planning to add new windows (or other glass panels) to your home, you should check local building regulations before proceeding.

Although safety glass may cost more, it need look no different from ordinary glass, will not affect your view or the availability of light, and will offer better safety than ordinary types of glazing.

Double glazing

Double glazing – where the window frame is fitted with two panes of glass with a small gap between them – offers reduction in noise levels, condensation and heat loss. There are two main types of double glazing: sealed unit and secondary sash. The first is formed of two panes of glass separated by dry air or other glass in an hermetically sealed unit. In the other type, a second pane in its own frame is secured to the existing frame.

With the latter type (that is secondary glazing), it is possible for condensation to build up between the two panes of glass, which can lead to fogging, damp, and conceivably, in extreme cases, wood rot, so it is preferable to choose conventional double glazing with sealed units if you can.

Types of glass suitable for double glazing are ordinary or annealed glass, low-emissivity glass, which is energy efficient and reflects heat back into the room, and safety glazing, such as toughened or laminated glass, as mentioned previously.

FAR LEFT: This re-inforced glass incorporates a fine metal mesh, which not only provides added security protection, but is also a guard against glass shattering in cases of accidental breakage.
TOP: This entertaining pictorial scene in stained glass does away with the need for a net curtain by obscuring the view, and provides colour and interest without restricting the flow of light.
ABOVE: Small diamonds of coloured glass in the centre of each panel break up a long expanse of plain glazed windows.

Stencilled Window

Stencilled glass obscures the view but gives a delicate, lace-like effect, which is attractive both inside and out. This pretty design is relatively easy to achieve, but you need a steady hand. Aerosol paint is water resistant, but avoid scratching the surface.
You will need: *stencil card, fine black pen, pencil, lace, photocopies, craft knife, spray adhesive, talc, newspaper, cutting mat, scissors, masking tape, white aerosol paint, protective mask for the nose and mouth.*

1 Using stencil card 30cm (12in) by 11cm (4½in), draw a line 1.5cm (½in) in from each edge. Draw shapes onto the card or use photo-copies of lace. Make sure that the design at both edges of the card match. To transfer a photocopy, turn the photocopy face down onto the stencil card and rub the back with a pencil, then draw around the shapes firmly onto the card. Go over the design with a black pen and fill in the shapes to be cut out with black lines to make it easier to see when cutting. Put the sten-cil on a cutting mat or sheets of newspaper and cut the shapes out using a craft knife.

2 Ensure that the window is clean and grease free. Apply spray adhe-sive to the back of the stencil and place it in the bottom left hand corner of the window and fix it in place with masking tape. Cut a 45 degree triangle from card and fix it in place over the lefthand corner of the stencil. Mask off the surrounding area with sheets of newspaper. Hold the can of spray paint about 25cm (10in) away from the surface and apply in short sharp 'puffs'. Remove masks and peel away the stencil. Reposition the sten-cil on the next area of window, matching up the ends of the design (you will need to be particularly careful at the corners, carefully applying the cor-ner triangle each time). Repeat as above until the border goes right round the window.

3 Measure the rectangle inside the border on the glass and cut a piece of lace to fit it exactly. Apply spray adhesive to one side of the lace and carefully position it on the glass. Stick a strip of masking tape all the way round the lace to act as a border, then mask off all the surrounding area with newspaper and tape. Spray as above. Remove masks, tape and lace. Blurred edges can be improved by gently scraping the paint away with a craft knife, but be careful not to scratch the glass.

Window Shelves

Glass objects, plants and trinkets can look wonderful when displayed on a table underneath a window, but they can look even better if arranged on shelves right in front of the glass in the window, where direct daylight will shine through or onto them. For example, a collection of Bristol Blue glass containers, old green glass lemonade or beer bottles, or perhaps delicately engraved or etched drinking glasses will all look luminous when light shines through them.

The light from the window provides a natural spotlight, emphasising the colour, sheen and shape of the object on which it shines. Metals such as silver, copper and brass will glow in sunshine, and even dark objects that have interesting shapes can look good displayed in

this way – they will be silhouetted by the back lighting from a window.

Plants such as spring bulbs, ferns and begonias will also look attractive arranged on window shelves and will thrive in the direct sunlight. Do be careful, however, that delicate foliage doesn't get frosted by being too close to the glass during cold winter months, and remember to water plants regularly during hot dry weather.

Window shelves are not only a good way to set off a collection of trinkets, but are also ideal for obscuring a dull or unpleasant outlook. If you have a basement room that looks out on another wall, for example, why not paint the wall white to reflect extra light back into your room and use window shelves to create an interesting feature instead of a blank outlook?

A room higher up in a building may have an outlook that is directly into another apartment or room, or onto an ugly array of TV ariels and satellite dishes. In cases such as these, window shelves provide privacy while still letting in the daylight.

The recess of the window frame provides the two upright struts needed to support shelves. You can use plain wooden shelves, painted to coordinate or match the colour of the frame and surround, or you could try incorporating glass shelves. The latter are best made from reinforced safety glass.

Glass shelves are unobtrusive and create an illusion that the objects resting on them are floating in the air. Glass shelves must be kept clean and unmarked; if they become opaque, they will lose their magical quality.

If you don't want to go as far as putting up shelves you can still use the window sill as a shelf and hang wind chimes or a decorative mobile from the top of the window frame. Or, particularly if you have a recessed window, why not create an indoor hanging basket?

WINDOW SHELVES

FAR LEFT: Certain plants thrive in direct sunlight and what better way to give them their fill of sunshine than to display them on shelves placed across the window.

LEFT: The window sill can also be used to show off a selection of interesting trinkets. Hang wind chimes or a mobile from the top of the window frame to obscure a dull view.

BELOW: Two long glass shelves provide an excellent display area for a collection of curios. Glass objects, especially coloured or patterned ones, will be highlighted when light shines through them.

Window Catches

Early window catches were two interlocking wooden sockets into which a peg was fixed, or leather thongs that were laced and tied through a wooden eye. These days catches are more sophisticated and can be adjusted to provide a variety of widths at which the window can be held open, thereby also acting as a security device, preventing windows being prized open.

ABOVE: This ornate catch is not only an attractive feature on a window frame, but it is also designed to be easily gripped in the palm of the hand. Although their purpose is practical, window catches are often designed to be decorative, too.
RIGHT: Large casement windows and French doors, which became popular in the Regency period, were closed by this type of catch. A long metal bolt, operated by an ornate central handle, locks into recesses in the top and bottom of the frame.

Window catches are often overlooked, but they are an important detail that can enhance the finished appearance of a window. Architects such as Lutyens and Voysey specifically designed window catches to complement their decorative schemes. Handles and catches can be ornate and attractive or plain and unobtrusive, so choose them to suit the type of window finish you wish to create, and try to retain the period style of the window.

There are a number of different locking devices, from the bolt and latch or lever handle to the more ornate central twist handle and rod, which fits into sockets at the top and bottom of the window frame, usually found on tall casement and French windows.

Catches don't have to be new – you may find interesting old or antique ones in salvage and reclamation outlets as well as in antique shops. Brass fittings can be revived to their former lustre with a good cleaning using a proprietary cleaning agent. Wrought-iron catches, found on old casements, mock Tudor and cottage windows, often end in a decorative curl. If well maintained and not allowed to rust, these durable catches should easily withstand the rigours of time, and even old ones tend to need little or no restoration.

The sash fastener, which secures the top and bottom halves of the window together, is usually a sliding, lever-style brass fastener, which has changed little since its invention in the eighteenth century. Screw bolts, though more time consuming to undo, give greater security.

A detail often found on sash windows are small recesses in the frame to give the hand a better purchase when sliding the windows up and down. In the late nineteenth century there was a fashion for embellishing these with ornate brass panels, thereby enhancing the appearance of the window as well as being a practical addition to the day to day use of the window.

Window Security

An unlocked window is an open invitation to a thief or trespasser, so secure fastenings are a necessity in every home and building. As well as conventional locks, there are now many special security devices available through specialist shops and hardware stores. These include window screws, which bolt through the over-

lapping frames of sash windows, and hooks that allow the window to be opened far enough to let air circulate, but not sufficient to give a burglar access.

Reinforced glass is another option, and is particularly useful in remote locations, where the sound of breaking glass may not arouse suspicion. It looks no different from ordinary glazing but has additional strength, which makes it less vulnerable to breakage.

Internal shutters also offer additional security. The old-fashioned folding panelled shutters, once used primarily as draught excluders, have the additional virtue of securing a home against a vandal coming through a broken window pane. American-style louvered shutters are more readily available and can be adjusted to vary the amount of light in the room, and they offer privacy as well. If a window is broken, their solid presence makes it much more difficult for an intruder to gain access.

Electric sensors can be installed to pick up movement in a room. The circuit is set when the house is empty and any movement – such as a window being smashed and opened – is detected by the sensor, which in turn triggers an alarm.

For upper windows, anti-climb paint can be applied to the sills and drainpipes, which will make it difficult, if not impossible, for a thief to hoist himself to that level.

Concertina metal shutters are another option. These can be fitted into the frame around the window and fold discreetly out of sight when not in use. The more conventional metal shutters are often not particularly attractive, but they are very effective.

More appealing than concertina shutters are decorative wrought-iron screens, which can be made to order by specialist foundries and blacksmiths. These ornate screens can be fitted internally, with hinges so that they can be folded out of the way, or externally, where they can be permanently fixed in place.

If you choose to have shutters as part of your security regime it is important that you instigate regular maintenance checks. The overall structure of the shutter should be well cared for and you will need periodically to repaint the wooden panels or louvres and apply rust-retardant paint to metal shutters. Hinges and locking devices should be kept well oiled and tightly screwed. Screw heads, especially on hinges on external walls, can be covered by small caps, which make them more difficult for a potential thief to unscrew.

FAR LEFT: Open windows can be an invitation to a thief even if you are at home. This type of safety lock secures an open window and is also a useful way of preventing small children from climbing out.

LEFT: American-style louvred shutters are both versatile and protective. They create a wooden screen inside the window, which may deter a burglar, and they can be folded back or adjusted to allow different strengths of light.

BELOW: The concertina metal screens seen in the first-floor windows of this house are not attractive, but they are effective as a deterrent. The screens can be folded back to the edge of the window frames and kept out of sight when not required.

Window Seats

Some window seats are created on an extra wide window sill; others are specially built into bay or bow recesses; some styles may stand proud of the wall under the window or even be a disguise for a radiator. Whatever its style or appearance, a window seat's primary purpose is generally to provide a comfortable resting place from which you can admire the view.

Large window seats are usually found in bay or bow windows and can seat several people at a time, or be used by one person for a leisurely lounge. Window seats can also be made to fit into the base of a narrow window, where they will offer a solitary perch.

Whatever type of window seat you have or wish to create, there will usually be a space underneath for storage. The box-like structure under the seat can be accessed by a door or doors at the front, or the seat itself can be hinged to form a lid.

In a child's bedroom, such underseat storage is an ideal place to stack away games and toys when not in use. In a bathroom, a window seat can be a restful place to enjoy the warmth and relaxation after a bath, while also providing a useful storage area for spare towels, tissues and bath preparations.

A window seat could also be built over and around an uninspiring radiator. The seat will not only create a decorative feature in the room, but will also provide a warm and comfortable place to sit. (Radiators are usually sited under windows, so that the hot air counteracts the cold air of surrounding the window.)

Dressings for a window seat are important, and you will need to decide whether to opt for fabrics that match the rest of the scheme in the room or to choose a contrasting material that will make the seat a feature. A narrow window and seat may best be dressed with a blind and a simple cushion, as the priority will be to keep the window as a source of light. With bigger bow-window seats, pelmets, generous curtains and several plump cushions will block only a small amount of the total light.

Ideally, window-seat cushions should be well padded, especially if the base underneath is stone or solid wood, which will not give when you sit down. If the surface on which the cushion is to rest is stone, you may consider making the bottom of the cushion cover out of felt or a similar thick fabric, which will also help with warmth.

If you don't have a recess or a deep sill in which to put a traditional window seat, why not simply place a bench under a window? Alternatively, you could create one by fixing a strong bench or shelf to the wall and covering it with a frilled valance and coordinating or matching cushions (see pages 34–35 for further details).

LEFT: This Shaker-style library is austere and simply decorated. The window looks out over a magnificent view of a church and surrounding countryside, but the seat is not designed for lingering.
TOP: This simple blind is an ideal way to make the most of a small window seat. The decoration is simple; there are no folds of curtain material to cramp the limited space available and the loose cushions are easily moved when the blind is let down.
ABOVE: This bow window has enough space to accommodate a more fancy dressing. A short gathered pelmet and generous curtains make it an inviting nook in which to sit and watch the world go by.

Window Seat Cushion

If you don't have a window recess, you can still place a suitable bench beneath a window. This comfortable window seat cushion with its pretty co-ordinating valance will enable you to use the area underneath to discreetly store books and boxes.
You will need: *fabric, co-ordinating fabric for valance, foam, thread, piping cord, scissors, needle, sewing machine, velcro, self-covering buttons, tape measure, pins.*

1 Measure the seat. Cut a piece of 6cm (2½in) deep foam to fit. Cut out top and bottom pieces of cloth to the size of the foam, adding 1.5cm (⅝in) all the way round. Measure and cut out a long strip, 9cm (3½in) wide, for the sides and front, adding 3cm (1¼in) seam allowance. Cut out 2 panels for the back, each measuring the length of the back and each 9cm (3½in) wide. Fold over 1cm (⅜in) along one edge of each of the back pieces. Press and fold over tan additional 1.5cm (⅝in). Pin, tack and stitch in place. Lay the back panels over each other right side to wrong side so that the overall width is 9cm (3½in). Pin, tack and stitch.

2 Sew the back panel to the long strip for the front and sides with right sides together. Press seams open. Cut strips of co-ordinating fabric on the bias, join them to form longer strips and fold in half widthways. Place piping cord inside the fold and pin, tack and machine sew. Lay the piping cord onto the right side of the top panel of cushion fabric with raw edges together. Start at the back of the cushion. Lay the fabric strip for the sides, back and front on top of that, ensuring that the back panel is in line with the back of the main piece of fabric. Pin, tack and stitch all the way round. Add piping to the bottom of the cushion and pin, tack and stitch this to the sides as above. Trim off excess fabric, turn the right way out and press. Fill the cushion cover with the foam and stitch velcro onto the back opening of the cushion. Cover buttons with the piping fabric and sew onto the cushion.

3 To make the valance, measure the height from the floor to the under-side of the seat and add 6cm (2½in). You will need 3 pieces of fabric this width, 2 pieces one and a half times the depth and one piece one and a half times the width of the seat. Cut 6.5cm (2½in) strips of co-ordinating fabric the length of each panel of fabric. With right sides together, pin, tack and stitch the strips to the bottom of the main panels. Press the seams open. Hem the right and left hand edges. With wrong sides together, fold the top edge over 1.5cm (⅝in), then 3cm (1¼in). Pin and tack in place. Stitch one line 0.5cm (⅛in) and another 2.5cm (1in) in from the top edge. Hem the bottom of the curtain. Screw eyelets into the corners of the under-side of the seat and thread curtain wires through the tops of the curtains. Attach the hooks onto the eyelets, ensuring that the wire is pulled taut.

Choosing Poles and Finials

Finishing touches and attention to detail are the professional elements that really finish a window dressing. There is no point in spending time, money and effort choosing or making wonderful curtains if you hang them badly on an inappropriate pole of mottled old wood, for example.

Consider the style of the window dressing you are creating and then look at the overall scheme of the room.

Do you have old dark wood furniture which could be echoed by a rich wooden pole with carved finials, or have you lighter, more contemporary furnishings that would work well with a fine iron pole with curled finials?

Also consider the weight and fabric of the curtains. Are they heavy rich damask with lining, interlining and braid that will require a sturdy, solid pole to hold them up, or are they a light voile that needs only a fine rod for support? The answers to these questions will help you make a decision about the weight, size and style of pole or rod that will best suit your needs.

The type of finish you choose for the top of your curtain will also influence your choice (see also pages 64–67). If you have a gathered finish and you want the curtain to butt up close to the ceiling for a floor to ceiling effect, a standard curtain track is the best option. If you choose a tab top for your curtain head, you will need a pole or rod for it to slide along. Bear in mind, too, that the rod will show through each of the crenellated sections, so it is important to choose an attractive pole. With a slotted heading, where the pole is slipped through a tube sewn into the top of the material, little or none of the pole will be seen, so you could opt for a less expensive, simple rod.

Once you have decided on the type of pole you feel is right for your room, mark on the wall where the fixture will be put, and measure for your curtains from that point (see page 54), remembering to take into account the finish of the curtain and the type of fixture that will be used to attach the curtain to the pole. For example, if you are using a pole with curtain rings, measure the drop of the curtain from the bottom of the ring. On the other hand, if you opt for curtain track, take the measurement from the top of the track, because the curtain should conceal the plastic runner.

Finials

Once you have decided on the type and style of the curtain pole you are going to use, it is time to turn your attention to the decorative details at either end of the pole – the finials. Finials come in hundreds of shapes and sizes, from wrought-iron swirls, shepherd's crooks and spears – reminiscent of the tops on old street railings – to traditional polished brass or wooden spheres, and even carved wooden fruits and seahorses, which may be handpainted or gilded.

LEFT: Decorative ends for curtains poles, known as finials, come in endless styles and variations, from simple wrought-iron curls to ornate carved wooden designs that are painted or gilded.
RIGHT: Curtain poles don't have to be smooth straight rods, they can be interesting, decorative features in their own right. Sliding wooden rings let curtains hang below these wavy poles.
BELOW: These traditional poles and finials are timeless classics that will suit most decorative schemes and curtain types, although the depth of wood colour should be chosen to complement the curtain fabric.

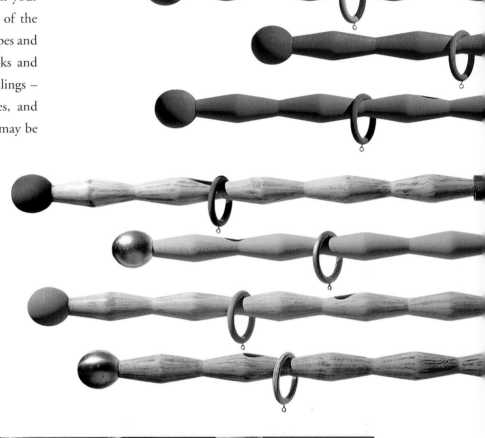

Contemporary designs include opaque glass rams horns, which look dramatic when light shines on them; twisted fine metal wire, which has an indefinite, uneven effect, and fragile looking open globes with threads of fine wire zig-zagging around the outside.

As with choosing a pole, you should select the finials to suit the overall scheme of the room, as well as making sure that they are of the right weight and size to complement the pole and the curtains. Themed finials such as a bunch of grapes or a seahorse are suitable for a kitchen and bathroom respectively; round or acorn-shaped polished wooden finials could be appropriate in a hall or study.

Try not to put very ornate finials with fancy patterned curtains in a room that is decorated with a heavily embossed or printed wallpaper; in such cases it would be better to opt for finials of a classical design or plain finish.

Tie-backs and bosses are used to drape the curtain back from the window, to create a gently curving sculptural shape instead of the straight up and down line of a plain hanging curtain. The finish you choose for the finial may influence your choice of boss. If you have selected a wrought-iron pole with a shepherd's crook finial, for example, you may like to repeat the crook's curve with a matching metal tie-back. The curtain need not be tied to this, but simply tucked behind it. Similarly, if you have wooden poles with acorn finials, acorn bosses will complete the set. (See pages 104–107 for more on tie-backs and bosses.)

The pattern of your fabric may also suggest a suitable finial. For example, if you have curtains with a repeat pattern of elephants, finials featuring carvings of elephant heads would highlight the theme. Similarly, gilded and bejewelled crowns would give a regal finish to heavy velvet curtains.

You could also try creating your own finials using various materials. On pages 40-41 we show how to make decorative finials from modelling clay, but depending on

the look you want to create, you could also try using papier mâché or fine wire mesh.

Papier mâché is simple and very cheap to make as well as being lightweight and easy to mould. The dried papier mâché shape can be painted or gilded, or you could use decorative coloured paper (tissue paper is good) to make it. Fine wire mesh can be scrunched, twisted or rolled into a shape and then attached to the end of the pole using lengths of wire wrapped around the pole end.

FAR LEFT: Contemporary designs for finials often use contrasting and unusual materials. These show fragile opaque glass used in conjunction with an iron rod, and twisted metal wire that has been repeatedly wound to create less definitive shapes than in traditional wrought-iron finials.
ABOVE: Tab-top curtain require smart poles , as even when the curtains are drawn the pole is still on show. These lightweight curtains have been hung on a fine iron pole which is finished with spear-shaped finials.

Decorative Clay Finials

Make your own unique finials and decorate them to complement your curtains. These lightweight pole ends are easy to make and can be simplified or embellished depending on your preference.
You will need: *curtain pole and fittings, petroleum jelly, self-hardening clay (not potter's clay), knife, paint, gold leaf, adhesive, fine paint brush, soft paint brush, steel wool.*

1 Apply a thin coat of petroleum jelly to the end of the curtain pole. For each finial, roll out a piece of clay so that it is approximately 8cm (3in) wide and long enough to wrap around the pole. Cut the edges of the clay to form a neat rectangle and place around the pole, leaving 1.5 cm (½in) clay to overlap the end of the pole. Press the clay around the pole and smooth off, joining the two edges of the rectangle together using a little water. Leave to dry. Shape another piece of clay into a ball by rolling between your hands. Pinch out the top to form a point. Keep the clay moist with water while working with it. Leave to dry.

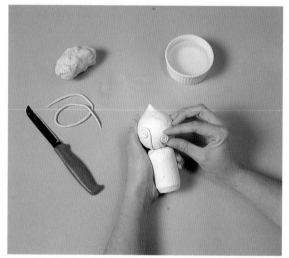

2 Remove the base of the finial from the pole and stick the conical shape to it with water. Apply a small piece of clay to the join if the two pieces feel insecure. Roll out long thin sausage shapes of clay, and curl at one end to form scroll shapes. Stick the scrolls to the finial, from the base up, alternating the direction of each scroll and pressing the bottoms into the base of the conical shape. Roll out a thicker sausage shape long enough to fit around the join and stick in place using water. Leave to dry completely.

3 Paint the finials and leave to dry. Brush adhesive onto the base of the finial and scroll shapes, ensuring the glue does not drip onto the area to be left ungilded. Leave to dry until tacky. Take a sheet of gold leaf and gently wrap around the finial. Brush with a soft brush to remove any excess gold. Rub the leaf with a soft paint brush and your finger tip to ensure firm adhesion. Gently rub steel wool over the gold area to give a slightly antiqued effect. Paint the curtain pole, rings and fittings to match and apply gold leaf, as described above, to the wall brackets.

CHAPTER 2

From the inside of a room, the windows are not only a primary light source, they are also an important decorative feature, and the way they are dressed will have an effect on the overall scheme of the room. In this chapter we take an in-depth look at the variety of ways in which a window can be dressed – from the lightest voiles and laces that can be used as a subtle screen, to the heavy damasks and velvets of more traditional styles.

Curtains and blinds – both plain and fancy – can be used alone or together in combinations that give a variety of effects. (For example, a roller blind can be teamed with

Looking Out

a light voile curtain, so that during the day the voile acts as a screen and soft light diffuser, while in the evening the roller blind can be drawn down to provide privacy.)

Practical instruction, such as how to measure for curtains and blinds, and how to extend old or second-hand curtains, is combined with lots of innovative ideas for making simple but effective window decorations without having to thread a needle. Finally, we look at all-important finishing details, such as pelmets and braids.

With the right choice of fabric, an attractive style and elegant finish, window dressings will enhance your home and make it a pleasure to be on the inside looking out.

Choosing Materials

When setting about the task of dressing a window, ask yourself a number of questions to help you determine the right fabric for your need. For example, does the window need to provide maximum light? How often will you need to cover the window? Often? – for example in a bathroom, where privacy will be expected on a regular basis. Occasionally? – for example in a sitting room, where privacy is only required in the evening when the room lights are on. The answers to these questions will help you determine what sort of window dressing will be most appropriate, and from there you can choose the right sort of material for the dressing.

For maximum availability of light look at fine ranges of voiles, nets and lace curtains (see also pages 48-49). For the bathroom, a permanent opaque screen will allow light into the room during the day, but still obscure the view. But, when electric lights are used in the evening, a dense dark curtain or blind could be pulled over the screen. For the sitting room, traditional curtains are a practical option because they can be drawn together when needed but pulled back to allow maximum light into the room during daylight hours.

The overall style of your room, including colours and patterns of other furnishings, will also give you a number of guidelines. For example, if the walls are covered with a richly patterned paper, it may be advisable to choose a plain curtain fabric; conversely, if the walls are plain, a patterned curtain may enhance the scheme. You should also take into consideration the coverings of upholstered furniture, bedspreads and headboards .

A kitchen or bathroom window, where the surrounding area is likely to be splashed with water or affected by steam, should be dressed with materials that can withstand that sort of wear. In areas such as these a roller blind may be better than a curtain, because the blind will

fit neatly against the window, whereas a curtain will hang in front, on the window surround, and be closer to taps, work surfaces and other potentially wet or messy areas. Blinds can also be easily rolled up and down as needed. For damp or steamy areas such as kitchens and bathrooms, it is a good idea, too, to look for specially treated fabrics that inhibit the growth of mould or mildew. Plastic and laminated materials, whose surface can be easily wiped dry, are another useful alternative.

TOP LEFT: The recessed window in this kitchen makes curtains a practical option as the material is away from the wet area of the sink. Easy-to-wash cotton gingham is an ideal fabric to use here.
BOTTOM LEFT: This neat, close-fitting roller blind is well away from the moisture of the bath. The fabric has been cleverly coordinated with the sea theme of the bath towel on the rail beneath.
ABOVE: With large windows you can afford to have more generous curtains; here the material complements the upholstery fabric.

Types of Material

The weight and type of material should be appropriate to the style of window dressing you wish to achieve. If you want a curtain that will drape around a boss and form a scoop or arch around the window, look at softer, pliable fabrics such as silk and light cotton. On the other hand if you intend to have formal, straight-hanging curtains, heavier fabrics, such as velvet or wool, will give the curtains gravitas and, with corner weights in the hems, they will hang vertically.

Starchy fabrics like hessian and raffia are best left to hang as straight and uncreased as possible. Fabrics with a 'stiff' handle – that is, which feel unyielding to the touch – will not hold a pleat well, so do not expect them to create regular or perfect folds when pulled back. Some fabrics can be deceiving – the natural and cream herringbone swatch shown on the opposite page looks as though it could be stiff, but is in fact made from silk and is very soft and easy to sew. It is always worth feeling a fabric rather than relying solely on looks.

As well as considering the weight and suitability of a material for the type of curtain or blind treatment you have in mind, you should also look at the colours and patterns of the fabric. Using the same palette of colours – ie shades darker or lighter with a hint more blue or red, for example – can be a successful plan.

The colour of your curtain and blind fabrics should also complement the upholstery, floor covering and wall colours in the room. If your room is already decorated and carpeted, it may be useful to take a swatch of upholstery fabric, sample card painted with the wall colour, and a small remnant of the carpet with you when you go to choose your materials. Better still, ask the shop to give you fabric swatches to take home so that you can test the material against the colours in the room, and also see how the pattern or design will work with the rest of the room and in different lights, ie by day and electric light.

It is worth taking a little time to try and test materials before you buy them – it is easy to think you know the shade of pink or blue you want, only to find, when you get the fabric home, that it is too peachy or too green.

TOP ROW (from left to right): *Moire*, refers to the watermark-style pattern woven into the material, often silk. *Brocade* or *jacquard* is an intricately woven fabric with figured designs. *Corded* or *ribbed cotton* is suitable for both curtains and, if retardant treated, upholstery. *Velvet* has a dense pile and can be made from silk, cotton or synthetic fibre, such as rayon or nylon. *Cotton drill* is sturdy and suitable for blinds and curtains.
MIDDLE ROW: *Cotton floral* with a soft, matt finish. Cotton floral *chintz* has a shiny glazed finish. Lightweight *wool* with a window-pane check. Dyed cotton *muslin*. Printed cotton *voile*.
BOTTOM ROW: Woven *raffia*, good for blinds. *Slub silk*, here in a herringbone weave, is in fact very soft and drapey. *Linen*, a medium-weight weave useful for curtains and blinds. Printed *hessian*, a coarse fabric made from jute. Finely woven *hemp* has a crisp handle, good for blinds.

Lace and Voile

From fine cotton muslin and finest organdie to nylon nets, these lightweight fabrics provide a shield from passing gazes yet allow daylight to pass through them and into the room.

Traditionally this type of curtain is white, but fashions have changed and coloured voiles have become increasingly popular. Whether you opt for a cream or antique effect by dipping the fabric into dilute tea or coffee, or for a stronger colour using a commercial dye, remember that the strength of colour is determined by the length of time and ratio of dye to water used.

Voiles can be decorated – some have patterns printed or woven into them, but you could try adding your own embellishments. Stencilling gold stars onto the surface or sewing brightly coloured threads roughly through the material are just two of a myriad of options. Voile type fabrics such as sari silk or mosquito netting are alternatives to the conventional ranges.

Because voiles are so light, they can be draped in unusual and decorative ways. A row of small brass hooks around the frame of an arched or gothic window can be used to hang a voile curtain. The curtain will fall in a way that mimics the shape of the frame but still blocks the view, at the same time allowing a diffuse light to shine in. You will also be able to see the decorative shape of the outline of the window.

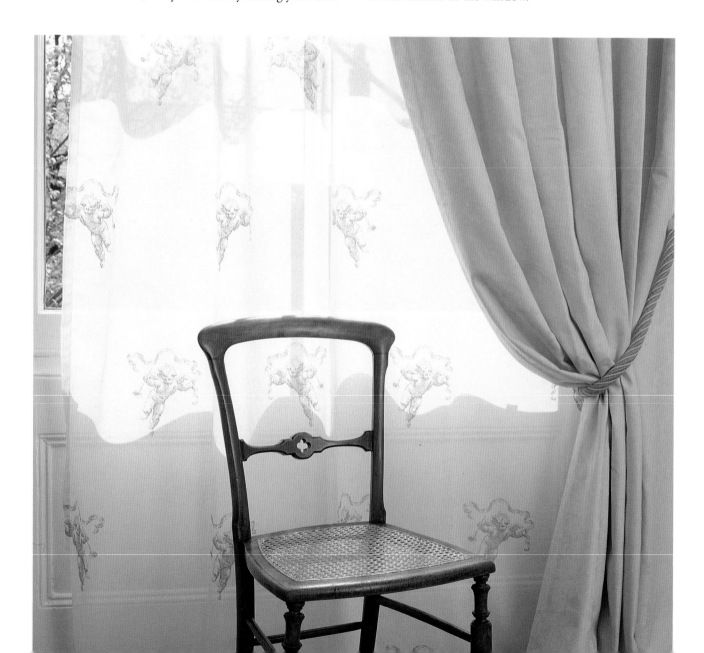

A length of voile could be draped around the outside of a curtain and even over a pelmet to give a softer and lighter appearance to a dark curtain. A voile curtain could also be draped around a window where a roller blind has been installed, which would give a finished pelmet effect to what might otherwise be a plain and fairly uninteresting surround.

Lace often comes in ready-made panels. This is because finer laces may fray and run if cut and not properly bound. Commercially finished lengths of lace are specifically woven to size and finished so there is no danger of unravelling.

If you do cut a length of lace to make a curtain, finish the edges by rolling a small hem and sewing it in place securely with a row of close stitching, or cover the edges with bias binding or ribbon and sew in place.

Lace panels and the half-size café curtains are popular throughout Europe, especially in France, where they often have a pictorial design, such as a pastoral scene or a garden of flowers, woven into the fabric. Narrow pieces of lace, not necessarily matching, can be hung at the top and bottom of a window to restrict the view.

FAR LEFT: This sheer curtain is decorated with a cherub motif. You could make a stencil design based on a pattern from outer curtains and print it on a sheer curtain for a coordinated look.
ABOVE LEFT: This voile has an unusual red fleck which makes it more interesting than a plain curtain. This sort of decoration can be added using a commercial dye or waterfast marker pen.
ABOVE: Lace and printed voile curtains are popular for small windows as they frame the window but allow light through.

Unusual Fabrics

Standard traditional curtain fabrics include chintz, damask, velvet and moire, which you can buy by the metre at department stores and specialist shops. But look a little further and you will find a whole host of different materials and hangings that will make interesting and unusual curtains. Taking another look at existing curtains may also give you some bright ideas for freshening faded or old window dressings. With a little imagination and skill you can create something new and interesting out of a curtain that was once dull.

For example, for a bathroom window, you could cut a plain coloured shower curtain down to size and decorate it. If your window is of such dimensions that the shower curtain can be cut in half and still be the right size, try doubling the curtain and sewing around the edge to create a large pocket. Divide the pocket shape into evenly spaced columns and sew them from top to bottom. Place a seashell or plastic fish into the bottom of each tube and sew a line of stitching above them horizontally so that the shells and fish are retained in individual pockets. Repeat the process until the curtain is full then sew along the top and add tape or other appropriate curtain fixing.

Heavyweight curtains

Rugs, mats and other floor coverings can also be used as curtains. You don't need to cut a carpet in half to make the traditional two-curtain window dressing – simply hang it so that it can be draped over to one side, and hold it in place with a boss or tie-back. Heavy materials such as rugs are best hung from a robust pole. Clip-top curtain rings will grip the edge of the rug and eliminate possible damage that might occur if fabric tape were stitched in place. These heavy window hangings will not ruffle or drape easily, but they should provide a good, dense blackout, retain heat and afford a certain amount of noise insulation.

Crewelwork, which is usually eastern in origin, very often from India, can also be used to create an interesting window treatment. The basic cloth is a natural cream cotton hopsack which is richly embroidered with woollen chainstitch in a kaleidoscope of colours. The material is heavy but soft, and benefits from the addition of a cotton lining. Any remnants or off-cuts from crewelwork curtains could be used to create attractive cushion covers.

There has been a vogue for natural fabrics in recent years, and this has seen a rise in popularity of rough linen, hessian and canvas curtains. These fabrics are usually plain in colour but the rough texture of the weave provides an interest on the surface of the cloth. They are usually hardwearing and will withstand constant use, but as their colours are natural, they are prone to fade if exposed to too much direct sunlight.

ABOVE: This heavy crewelwork curtain has been backed and edged with a dark, complementary coloured material that highlights the delicate needlework of the panel.
RIGHT: The natural hessian fabric used for this side-swept drape complements the flooring in the room and the open weave allows a small amount of light to pass through.

Some manufacturers of curtain material use dyes that are less prone to fading, but if you hang an ethnic or antique kelim or dhurrie in a window, sunlight will most likely effect it. To prevent damage to the hanging, a discreet roller blind can be used to cut down direct light. Changing the hanging around will also help balance the fading effect. If you use clip-on rings, you can simply unhook the rug , turn it round and re-hang it, or, if you are using a pole, slide the hanging along to the other end so that it drapes in the opposite direction.

Tweed and wool tartan fabrics are heavyweight but attractive and tend to be used in living rooms and studies, where they will help in keeping in warmth. These more robust woollen materials will fold and drape more easily if backed with a good cotton lining.

Revitalising old fabric

You could try reviving existing curtains with quilting, appliqué and stencilling. Material that has gone limp or lost its crisp chintz finish can be given a boost with quilting; you can either quilt all over the curtain or pick out a specific motif and repeat the quilting each time the motif appears. Separate the curtain from its lining and place a layer of commercial terylene wadding, or an old light-coloured blanket between them. (If you use a blanket, remember that the curtain should not be machine washed, but will require professional dry cleaning).

When the three layers are level and square, tack and then stitch the outer edges so that the 'sandwich' of materials stays firmly in place. With a checked or striped fabric, sew through the three layers of material by following the lines of the printed pattern. To create a more random quilted pattern, sew round the outline of a motif, such as a flower or a bird, that is repeated at regular intervals.

Appliqué is an effective way of covering blemishes or stains on a curtain or adding interest to a plain voile. For example, a silhouette in black fabric of the Manhattan skyline could be enhanced with glass beads and sequins sewn along the base of a curtain as though they were the city lights. Or felt leaves could be scattered randomly to look as though they were falling from a tree above.

In a child's room cut-out numbers or letters can be instructional as well as decorative and in the bathroom you could cut out fish or sea-shell shapes from shiny fabrics and sew them around the edge of plain curtains to give them a lift.

Stencilling is a quick and easy way to bring pattern to a plain fabric. You can use a fabric dye or a specialist felt pen in the same colour to create the pattern and choose either a darker shade than the material or one that is a contrast. On white voile a simple pattern in a matt gold or silver paint can look very effective. Ready cut stencils can be bought from stationary and department stores, or you can cut your own from a sheet of stiff board. Stamping is also becoming popular, is easy to do, and again, you can buy the stamps or make your own.

LEFT: Here, a plain white sheer curtain has been stencilled with a repeated classical motif. Such a decoration is fairly easy to achieve, very effective, and, of course, unique.

TOP RIGHT: Sari silk comes in a rainbow choice of colours, plain and patterned. The soft drape, and long single length of the silk makes it ideal light-weight window dressing in a room that does not require a blackout.

RIGHT: A child's cotton bedspread has been recycled as a light curtain in this bathroom. Cotton bedcovers and tablecloths can easily be adapted to become window covers instead. If a table cloth is stained or damaged hide the blemish with an appliqué or stencilled design.

How to Measure for Curtains

It is important to be careful and accurate in your measurements for curtains, to avoid buying a surplus of material as well as to ensure that you have enough to complete the project. If you are dressing a recessed window, you can make the window seem larger by dressing it outside the recess. A small window on a flat wall can be made to appear larger if the curtains are pulled right back to the edges of the frame. If you do this, you will need to allow additional width on your fabric measurements.

If you choose a patterned material, measure the distance between each repeat of the pattern and allow extra material, so that you can adjust each width of material to match the repeat of the pattern. It is advisable to allow an extra complete pattern repeat on each length of material so that you have extra fabric with which to line up the pattern on each curtain.

To work out the length of fabric needed for the curtain, mark out where pole or rod will be, or better still, fix it in place. If you are using curtain hooks, remember to measure from the bottom of the hook, ie from the point where the material will touch the hook.

For a gathered heading to be used on a track, take the measurement from the top edge of the track, as you will need to allow material to cover the width of the track. For tab-top curtains, measure from where the body of the curtain will hang beneath the tab, but remember to add extra for the fabric needed to make the tabs themselves. For pocket headings, add in an allowance for the fabric required above the pole, as well as additional material to make the pocket (ie the width of the pole plus a couple of centimetres for easy movement).

From the pole or rod, measure to the sill for a short curtain, to below the sill, but above a radiator, for a medium-length curtain, and to the floor for a long curtain (shown as **B**, **C** and **D** in the diagram). To the overall length you will need to add allowances for turnings at the heading and the hem – a rough guide is 16cm (6in) for the hem and 5cm (2in) for the top.

For the width of a curtain, the general rule is to measure the width of the window and double it. This gives fullness to curtains with ruffled or gathered tops. For leaner curtains, one and a half times the width of the window will be adequate.

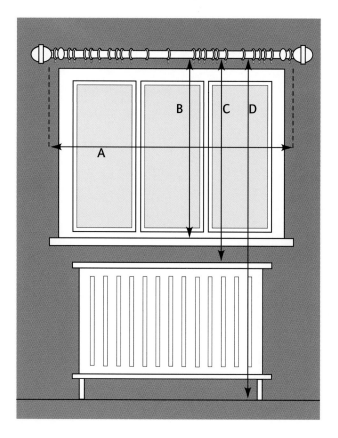

LEFT: Measurements for the width of the curtain should be taken from inside the finials of the pole (**A**). This measurement should be doubled to give the right amount of fabric for generously pleated curtains. For the length, the measurement should be adjusted to suit the type of heading to be used. The drop should then be measured to the sill (**B**), above the radiator (**C**), or floor length (**D**).
RIGHT: These curtains fit neatly within the frame of the window and do not interfere with the furniture in front.

Curtain Treatments

The style of curtain treatment you choose will be influenced by a number of things, such as the shape and size of your window, whether the window stands alone or in a group, the style of decoration of the rest of the room, and the desired function of any curtains.

Period curtain treatments

If you have a period style house or are following an historic decorative theme, your choice of window dressing will also be affected by the furnishings and fabrics appropriate to that time. A simple guideline for fabrics and finishes suitable for the major decorative periods are described below, but for more detailed references look at paintings or pictures of the era or visit historic houses that have been decorated in period style.

Tudor-style interiors best suit tapestry, dark velvet, rich damask or crewelwork curtains, and these should be generous in proportion, simply gathered or tab topped and supported by wrought-iron rods. Strictly speaking, Tudor homes did not have curtains, but for modern-day comfort you will probably want to include them.

Georgian houses or rooms should have panelled shutters, but where these do not exist, moires, damasks or large but simple bird or animal prints in mid-strength colours will suit. Window dressing also started to become more fancy during the Georgian period, and fringes, swags and pelmets are all appropriate additions.

Lace, velvet, deep fringes, ornate braids and tassels are all important features of Victorian window dressing style. Full-length, theatrically draped curtains with gathered tops, fringed edging, substantial pelmets and tie-backs are all correct.

For contemporary interiors, which often have very large windows, simple curtains, perhaps of natural shades of linen with tab tops, or layers of opaque voile, may be the most effective solution, especially if you want to create a light, airy feel and informal look.

Deciding on length

As well as the arrangement of the curtains – simple and unlined, or rich velvet with all the trimmings – the length of the drop of the curtain will influence the finished look. Floor-length curtains tend to be more formal, whereas short ones have a more casual appearance.

Curtains that reach the floor can skim the surface of the carpet or boards, while those with a generous overflow will drape along the skirting board in a languid

FAR LEFT: These generous voile curtains flow onto and along the floor for a grand effect. This light and airy, but stylish look can be achieved cheaply with inexpensive fabrics such as cotton muslin and synthetic organdie.

ABOVE: Two narrow fake curtains and a central sheer fill the window in an unusual, but very simple arrangement.

LEFT: For this feminine bedroom, an ornately decorated pelmet and ruffled floral curtains are the perfect choice. Tie-backs create a gentle drape at the curtain edges.

curl. Short curtains are more appropriate for small narrow windows or windows with a radiator beneath. If a long curtain drapes to the floor over the front of a radiator, much of the heat given off will be trapped behind it rather than circulating in the room.

The way that the top of the curtain is gathered, pleated and attached to the rod or pole will affect the drape and hang of the material. A slotted heading, where the pole is inserted into a fabric tube sewn into the curtain, is ideal for a draped arrangement. The top of the curtain will not be pulled apart but will stay as a solid pleated line along the pole. The sides of the curtain can be draped back and held with tie-backs to form a sculpted frame around the window.

Tab-top, tie or loop-headed curtains do not require as much fabric as those with a gathered finish. In fact, if tab-top curtains are made in fabric that is too heavy and with too much material, they will be difficult to draw along the pole, and the fabric loops will ruche and drag.

Combining curtains and blinds

Layering curtains and blinds creates a more versatile and interesting window dressing, but you will need to plot out carefully how and where each layer will be attached to the window, and which heading will work in conjunction with another.

There are a few combinations of blinds and curtains, and curtains with curtains, that can cause difficulties or unsightly overlaps of material. For example, there is no point in putting a tab-top curtain on top of a ruched voile, as the puckered heading of the voile will appear bunched and cluttered behind the tab top.

A useful arrangement of curtains that ensures they don't become tangled is to attach the voile or lighter curtain on the window frame or in the recess of the window and hang the heavier outer layer from a pole or runner fixed to the face of the wall in front of the window.

When planning a combination of curtains and blinds, work out what you need from the window during both

LEFT: A short tailored curtain fits neatly into the recessed window in this bathroom. The frilly pelmet complements the decorative floral print of the fabric, but is not so fussy as to be overpowering.

RIGHT: Two types of curtain have been put together to create a variable window covering. The half, or café, curtain at the bottom provides privacy at all times while the upper curtain can be drawn to allow extra daylight into the room.

BELOW: With plain material you can add embellishment with trims. Here, big bow tie backs, an ornate pelmet and underfrill have a striking effect.

the day and night. If the window is on the sunny side of the apartment or house, do you want a roller blind to cut down the glare and bleaching effects of the sun? A blind has the advantage that it can be easily and quickly rolled up out of sight when not in use. Alternatively you could use a full- or half-length voile or net curtain, which will diffuse the light and also protect fabrics and floor coverings from fading.

If you like a clear window or enjoy the view, a blind is probably the answer, but if the view is unsightly, or you need privacy, then a curtain could be the solution.

From the blind or voile work outwards. If you have opted for the blind, do you like the clean, neat-fitting appearance of it alone, or do you see it purely as a practical solution? Whether you choose a blind or a voile curtain, ask yourself if you have the space to add extra curtains or will the soft drape of fabric over the curtain pole or pinned to the window frame be enough? Will another layer of heavier curtains add to the overall decoration in the room?

You may find it useful to mock up the window you are to dress by drawing it to scale on paper and trying out various combinations and effects by layering up swatches of the fabrics you intend to use.

Outer curtains

The outer layer of curtains can be made in many shapes and weights. The simplest are false curtains – just a width of fabric that is put in place for effect rather than use. If the curtain is purely decorative, ie around a hall window where the curtain need never be drawn, a small, curtain, using just enough material to create narrow pleated side borders, is ideal.

A current trend with voile and organdie curtains is to layer them, with contrasting colours placed one in front of another. Where the curtains are single the colours remain true, but where they cross a third shade appears – for example red and yellow curtains will create orange where they overlap.

Mid-weight fabrics commonly used for curtains include jacquard, silk, taffeta, damask and cottons, such as chintz with its shiny resin finish, and calico toile de jouy with its distinctive single-coloured pastoral designs. These fabrics are suitable for most decorative schemes and can be left in a classic drape to fall straight from the pole or rod, or can be swept back with ties or bosses.

The heavier materials such as velvet and the array of woollen cloths may mark if draped or tied back so they are best left to hang straight, and these bulkier heavy fabrics will crowd smaller windows, so are more suitable for larger, formal types.

When using plain or self-patterned fabrics, such as taffeta or damask, you can afford to trim curtain edges, tie-backs and pelmets with a matching or contrasting piping, frills or decorative braid. Use the plainness of the material as a background on which to add decoration. It

TOP LEFT: The checked roller blinds have been linked into the overall scheme by adding matching tie-backs to the curtains as well as a cushion and upholstered stool in the same material.
RIGHT: Alternate curtains in plain and checked fabric are an interesting change from having all four curtains in the same material.

can be very effective, and a checked roller blind can be made an integral part of a window scheme by adding a matching border of the blind fabric to the curtains.

Shutters negate the need for curtains as they perform the same functions of keeping out light and providing a screen, but if you need daylight and privacy when the shutters are open, you could fit a roller blind within the window frame. The unobtrusive roller blind can be discreetly rolled out of view when not in use, and will not interfere with the attractive classic lines of the shutter.

The finished look

As a rule, if a window or windows are large and a major feature in a room, then their decoration and dressing will be an important feature in the overall scheme. The richer, heavier and more ornate the materials used, the grander the finished effect will be.

However, it is worth remembering that it is easier to start with a simple scheme and add to it, than to have a fussy design and dismantle it. If you are unsure of how a finished dressing may look, start with the most simple combination and build it up. If you can draw, sketch out the various combinations of blinds and curtains, with pelmets, tie-backs or bosses and see how they look. You may also find it helpful to build up a small pinboard of sample swatches of material so that you can have a more tangible idea of how the colours and patterns will relate.

the curtain material is densely patterned – a toile de jouy or a Provençal print, for example – keep the trimmings simple and opt for a plain trim rather than anything too colourful or fancy.

Interesting and unusual effects can be created by mixing and matching fabrics, but be sure that the materials are of compatible weights. A light voile border on a heavy wool curtain will look odd, for example.

Plain curtains with a patterned border or visa versa

FAR LEFT: This plain curtain is decorated with an unusual fringe pelmet. The generous drape of the material is swept majestically to one side and hooked behind a tie-back, creating a stylish, sculptural appearance.

TOP LEFT: The roller blind is the practical part of this window dressing; the outer dressing is a decorative extra.

ABOVE LEFT: These Regency striped drapes accentuate the height of the windows, and the horizontal sweep of the fabric creates an illusion of width.

Curtain Headings

The way in which the top and bottom of a curtain are finished will affect the way it hangs and how it lies against the window frame or opening. For example, a flat finish top like a tab or loop will give a flush or slightly undulating effect, whereas gathered or pleated finishes will create curtains with volume.

Tracks and poles should be chosen to suit the type of top you have on your curtains, as well as the style you wish to create. For example, a gathered curtain top will work on most fittings, including standard and overlapping track, or poles and rods with rings, but a tab-top curtain will need a simple pole or rod.

Gathered headings

Most gathered headings are achieved with a commercially produced tape, which has one, or more usually two, rows of fine cord stitched evenly along it. Sew the tape securely onto the back of the finished, flat curtain, then, holding the cords firmly at one end, ease the fabric along them until it is evenly pleated.

The tape backing on a ruffled curtain comes with integral fabric pockets into which to slot the curtain hooks. Final tweaking, ie pulling the cords in a little to make the curtains narrower, or loosening them a bit to allow more width, can be done once the curtains are up, which is especially useful if you have overlapping track. But don't forget, once you have finished your final adjustments, to make sure that you tie the ends securely, so that the gathers don't loosen with wear. Curtains with a gathered heading are suitable to go under a pelmet.

Hand-pleated headings

Many more formal types of pleats can be made without the use of commercial curtain tape, but these headings are more labour intensive as the pleats have to be made by hand. A stiffener called buckram is used to make the top of the curtain more manageable. The curtain fabric at the head of the curtain folds over the buckram, which comes in standard widths of 10cm and 15cm (4in or 6in). (Remember to allow extra fabric for this fold when you are measuring for the length of the curtain.)

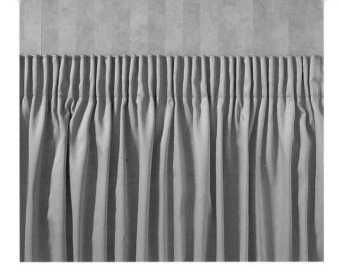

Sew the buckram securely into place onto the flat curtain fabric. Decide on the width of the pleat you want by wrapping the fabric in a loop around your fingers – up to three fingers width will create a regular-sized pleat. When you have settled on a size, unwrap the material from your fingers and measure the width of fabric used to recreate the pleat. Then, using tailor's chalk or pins, mark out the pleat measurement on the reverse of the fabric until you reach the end of the material. Using the marks or pins as guides, re-trace your movements over the curtain top, wrapping the fabric around your fingers to create the pleats. As each pleat is formed, pin or tack it in place. When the whole curtain is pleated, fix the pleats permanently by sewing vertically down the back of each one to form a single tube shape.

There are a number of variations that you can try once you have formed the single pleats. For example, the goblet pleat is made by pinching in the base of the sewn tube below the bottom edge of the buckram. The pinched fabric is neatly sewn together and the result looks like a small wine glass or goblet. To hold the goblet shape, stuff a small piece of interlining or similar fabric

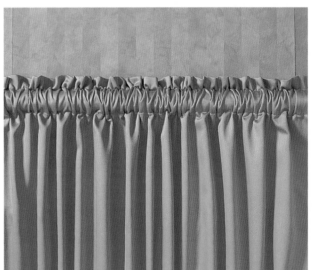

LEFT: Tie tops for curtains can be made from the same materials or in contrasting fabric, ribbon, tape or braid. These pretty tie finishes complement the soft decorative design of the curtain material. **RIGHT (top to bottom):** A *standard pleat* made using a commercially produced tape. A *pocket* or *channelled heading*, where the curtain pole is completely covered by the material. There is no need for hooks or rings, the material simply slides along the pole. *French pleats* are made by dividing one large pleat into three smaller ones. These *hand-pleated goblet pleats* have been made from a standard single pleat, which has been gathered at the bottom. The gather is highlighted with a contrasting button.

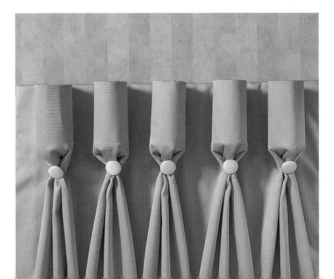

into the base of the goblet so that it stands proud of the flat face of the curtain.

A single large pleat can also be sub-divided into smaller pleats. Pinch in and sew the bottom of the pleat where it meets with the lower edge of the buckram. Flatten the top of the pleat out and insert three pencils, then tuck the material in on either side of the centre pencil to form three small equal pockets. Pin the folds on either side of the middle pencil to the back of the

pleat. Remove the pencils and stitch the fabric in place, then remove the pins and with your finger gently ease out the tops of the three small pleats.

Pocket headings

Pocket headings are used with poles or rods. A long, single pocket is created along the width of the fabric at the top. When the pocket is finished, the curtain pole is fed through until it is covered, except for a small length

66

at either end for fixing into brackets. The curtain is then pulled back along the pole and soft pleats are formed as the fabric ruches around the pole.

The pocket must be larger than the pole so that the fabric will run easily when pulled along. Lay the pole a few centimetres from the top of the curtain and fold the top edge over the pole, adjusting the fabric around the pole until there is sufficient to cover and a little extra for easy movement. Pin the turned-over edge of the curtain to the back and remove the pole. Sew in place. Thread the pole through and hang.

Flat headings

Flat headings such as tab- or tie-tops involve making loops along the top of the curtain at regular intervals. The loops can be made from the same material as the curtain, from contrasting colours or fabrics, or from materials such as ribbon, rope, cord or tape.

Measure the width of the curtain and divide into regular sections, about 16cm (4in) apart. You can sew strips of material to either side of the curtain top and tie them in a knot or bow around the pole, or alternatively, use single lengths of fabric to make loops through which to thread the curtain rod.

Another simple way to finish curtains is to make holes at even intervals along the top, finishing them with either overstitching or brass rivets, so that fabric will not rip during use. You can pass a rod or pole through the holes, or hang the curtain a few centimetres below the pole, lacing them together with cord, ribbon or rope.

Curtain hems

The bottom of a curtain can be simply hemmed, but if you add small metal weights inside the hem of the curtain, it will hang smoothly and vertically. Weights are particularly useful in lightweight curtains such as lace and net, as they will help to keep the curtains from blowing around when the window is left open.

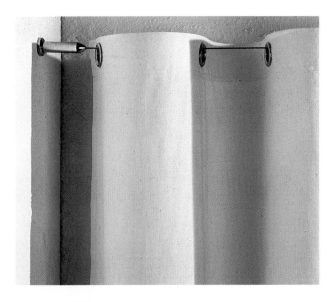

LEFT: An intricate smocking top gives these curtains an interesting finish. The curtains remain together at the top, emphasising the pattern made by the rows of neat stitching .
TOP: Rivets have been used to protect the holes in the top of this curtain, which could be cut or damaged by constant rubbing along the taught wire from which they are hung.
ABOVE: Weights sewn into the hems of curtains will make them hang tautly from the pole. A contrasting lining makes an unusual detail.

Blinds

Blinds are versatile and useful window dressings, providing a simple but effective way of blocking out light and obscuring a view. They are generally adjustable, so that the degree of light that passes through the window and into a room can be fine tuned to suit requirements. A single blind can be used in a small window or several blinds can be placed side by side across a wider opening.

Fitting neatly into a window frame or hanging just in front, blinds can usually be made from a fraction of the material required to make a curtain. If you have a small, but precious piece of material you would like to use, or can only afford a metre or two of a beautiful but expensive material, a simple screen blind could be the perfect way to make good use of it, as well as to show it off and is easy to make.

As blinds can be tailored to be exactly window size, they are ideal for small rooms, as they take up less space than curtains. They are also useful in bathrooms and kitchens, above or near wash basins or sinks, where water may be splashed about.

A blind can also be adapted to suit any scheme. From the most understated, simple cream calico roller, or a folding Roman blind to a fancy ruched blind with a decorative edge and tasselled pull or a scalloped edged quilted blind, the choice is yours.

Blinds can be used alone or in conjunction with curtains or a pelmet and can be made in most weights of fabric, barring bulky tweeds and heavy woollen fabrics that would be difficult to roll or gather up in folds. Even soft fabrics with a limp handle can be stiffened with special sprays and used in most styles of blind.

Roller, Roman, cascade, Austrian festoon and Venetian – there is a wide variety of blind styles which can be made in all sorts of different materials, from fine cotton to black-out material (useful in children's rooms), and from plain natural linen to ornate, gold-threaded brocades. Choose the style of blind to show your chosen material to its best advantage as well as to suit the size and shape of the window and the rest of the scheme in the room. Over the next few pages, we look at the options, discuss the best to use in various situations and give advice on how to choose appropriate fabric.

LEFT: This fine striped roller blind is simple but effective. It fits neatly into the window recess and does not get in the way of the screen to the right. The blind is easily rolled up when not in use.
RIGHT: Austrian blinds have more material and drapes than a roller blind. They are softer and more decorative but, like other blinds, can be confined to a limited area, such as above a radiator.

How to Measure for a Blind

Because most blinds are raised and lowered by means of cord pulleys it is important that they are as straight and true to the window frame as possible. However, as many window frames, especially those in older houses and cottages, are not exactly 'square', it is best to make the hangings for your blind as correct as possible to the wall rather than to the window itself.

For windows that have fanlights or rounded tops, it is best to start your blind below the arch. Tape a length of string or cord across the bottom of the arch and check it is straight with a spirit level. This line will provide a level marker from which to measure.

Mark where your batten or pole will be – either inside the frame, on the frame itself, or on the wall (see right) – and take the measurement for the drop of the blind from that point. If your blind is to cover the whole of the window, including the frame, measure from the outer limits of the frame all the way round. If, on the other hand, the blind is to fit snugly into the window, measure inside the frame. In both cases, remember to add extra for hem allowances and headings.

When you have decided on the style of blind and where it will be fixed, you will need to calculate the amount of fabric you need according to the type of blind. For example, a roller blind is flat, so the fabric required will be the size of the window with allowances for fixing to the batons and hems.

For a festoon blind, which creates its ruched appearance from its length as well as its width, you will need fabric approximately one and a half times the width of the window and, for four swags, double the length of the window. For Austrian blinds, which gather their pleats from the width, you will need fabric between one and a half and two and a half times the width of the window and to add approximately 30cm (12in) extra on the length, plus hem allowance. Cascade blinds are less full

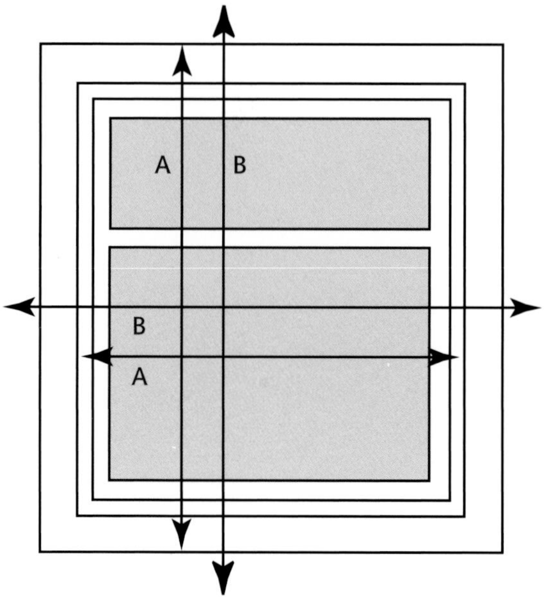

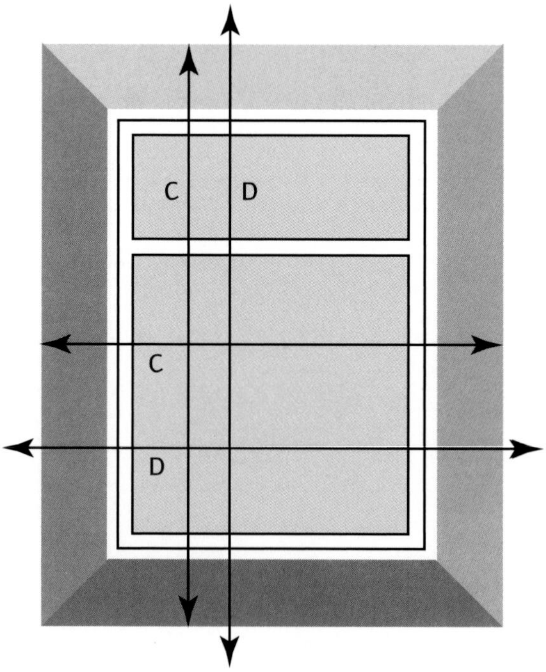

TOP: How to measure for a blind that will hang inside the frame of a window (**A**) or to the outside edge of the frame (**B**). The latter can make the window appear larger. **BOTTOM:** In a recessed window, a blind can either fit neatly to the window (**C**) or hang flat against the wall (**D**).

than the previous two types, but will need about 24cm (9½in) extra on the drop and an extra 3cm per 50cm (1¼in per 20in) on the width.

The length of fabric you will need for Roman blinds will depend on how many folds you want and of what size. For example, if you want five folds, each 25cm (10in) wide (ie 12½cm/5in when doubled) then add 25cm x 5 = 125cm (10in x 5 = 50in) to the window length, and then allow for heading and hem.

ABOVE: This leaf print roller blind fits neatly into the window surround. When fully pulled down, the blind should stop just inside the bottom of the frame and when rolled back it will take up a minimal amount of space.

Fancy and Ruched Blinds

Austrian, festoon and cascade blinds are among the most decorative of blinds, their ornate appearance being created by folds or gathers of ruched fabric. This style of blind can be traced ,back to the eighteenth century, when they were used for decorative rather than practical purposes (most windows at that time were fitted with robust wooden shutters).

Austrian and festoon blinds achieve their fullness from the material in the width of the blind; gathers or pleats are formed as the cords fixed to the back of the blind are pulled, raising up the bottom of the blind. A festoon blind also gets its drape from the amount of fabric in its length, so that as the blind is drawn up, the fabric 'backs up' from the bottom in rows of pleats. Cascade blinds are not as full, and do not require so much fabric (see page 74 for details of how to make one).

To achieve the best drape and fullness, soft, pliable materials, such as silk or lightweight cotton, are the best to use. A number of unusual effects can be achieved by layering fabrics one over another. For example, a layer of fine muslin over a strongly coloured floral print will create a softer look to the underlying cloth and, when drawn up and ruched, the muslin will appear as a pale, almost cloud-like facing to the blind. Layers of different coloured voile can be built up to create a single strong colour. For example, shades of yellow and blue can be placed one on top of another and sewn to form a single blind, which, when ruched, will give the appearance of a green blind that varies in shade and depth of colour.

If the purpose of the blind is to obscure a view but not to cut out light, use pale materials with little or no pattern and it will not be necessary to line the blind. If, on the other hand, the blind has a decorative rather than useful role, you could choose a patterned fabric and line and trim with a contrasting material.

These blinds are raised and lowered by a cord and ring arrangement. Several fine cords run vertically along the back of the blind and are held in place by numerous small rings. The cords are usually evenly placed across the back of the blind right to the outer edges to ensure that the blind draws up level, but they can stop a few centimetres from either end so that when the blind is drawn, the edges drape down in decorative tails.

The tops of these fancy blinds can be finished in a similar way to curtains with pleats or gathers. A pocket or channelled heading is ideal because the pole will be covered, and as the blind will never be drawn to the side like a curtain, the pole pocket can be a neat fit.

When a ruched blind is fully drawn up it looks similar to a draped pelmet (see pages 100-101) and could be used in conjunction with a plain roller blind to create a double blind window feature.

The bottom edges of these fancy blinds can be decorated as well, with frills, tassels, braids or fringing. And, of course, you could also add a decorative tassel or bead to the pull cord. You could create your own cord decoration by making a pompom from three or four shades of wool or silk threads.

LEFT: This festoon blind is perfect for a bathroom window; its full, generous furls create a decorative appearance at the window, yet it can be easily adjusted to suit day and night time needs.
ABOVE: Fabric ties hold these blinds up, rather than the cord and ring method used on most fancy blinds. Here the drop of fabric is gathered up by hand and secured in place with ties attached to the top.
RIGHT: The edge of this contemporary blind has been left loose and ungathered to create a deep, decorative border at the bottom of the blind. A simple scalloped edge is not difficult to make and gives a neat finish.

Cascade Blind

A cascade blind is a practical, as well as a pretty, solution for a small window where a curtain may be trapped behind furniture, such as in this bedroom. A fancy blind like this would also give a luxurious feel to a bathroom.
You will need: *fabric, lining, tape measure, scissors, pins, needle, thread, sewing machine, velcro, glue, small brass rings, wooden baton, brass eyelets, tacks, hammer, cord, brackets, wooden bead.*

1 Measure the window frame. Cut out a piece of fabric to the size of the frame, adding 20cm (8in) on each side, 12cm (4½in) to the bottom, and 8cm (3in) at the top. Make sure that any pattern on the material is centred. Fold over 20cm (8in) of fabric down the sides and 12cm (4½in) along the bottom and press. Open the folds out again and fold the corner point over until the point of the pressed fold meets the fold of the corner. Fold the sides and bottom of the fabric over again. Trim away excess fabric from the mitred corner. Press. Pin and hand stitch sides, bottom and corners.

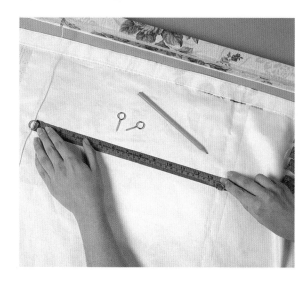

2 For the lining, measure a piece of fabric to fit from the hem lines on the right and left edges of the blind fabric, and from the very top of the fabric to the hem line of the bottom, then add 8cm (3in) to the width and 4cm (1½in) to the length. Fold over 4cm (1½in) along the sides and bottom of the lining fabric, then lay it on top of the blind, matching the folds with the stitched edges. Pin and hand stitch in place, then press with an iron. Fold over 8cm (3in) along the top of the blind, tucking the raw edge under. Press, pin and tack. Pin and tack a strip of velcro to this and machine stitch.

3 Mark a central line down the blind and another on either side two thirds of the way from the centre to the edge. of the blind Measure, mark and pin in 30cm (12in) intervals from the bottom to the top of each line. Sew brass rings in position at the pin points. Cover the baton with blind fabric, using glue, and tack the other side of the velcro to the front. Line up the baton with the blind top, mark 3 points on the underside, in line with the brass rings, and screw eyelets into the wood. Attach the baton to the window frame with brackets and attach the blind to the baton, matching velcro strips. Cut three lengths of cord, knot a length to each of the bottom rings of the blind. Thread the cords through the rings in a straight line so that all three pieces of cord come together on the right hand side. Fasten with a bead.

Plain and Roller Blinds

Less ornate (and requiring less fabric) than the Austrian, festoon and cascade blinds are the Roman, roller blind and gathered blinds.

Roman blinds

Roman blinds are made by sewing fine supports or rods at regular vertical intervals across the back of the blind. If the blind is to be lined, the rods can be covered in the lining fabric and sewn through to the front; if no lining is to be used, the rods should be covered in a plain, pale material. Small metal or plastic rings are sewn along each rod so that the cord, which is attached to the bottom of the blinds, runs through the rings in straight vertical lines. Roman blinds should not be made overly wide or the supports or rods may start to sag or bend.

Roller blinds

Roller blinds are best made with a commercially produced kit as the spring fixing required to rewind the blind would be difficult to make. Most department stores and specialist shops sell the kits, which come with making up instructions, rods for the top and bottom of the blind, brackets and a cord.

Ideally, fabrics for roller blinds should have some 'body', ie be slightly stiff or starched. Roller blinds are sometimes referred to as Holland blinds because strong Holland linen was used for making them. If you plan to make your roller blind from a soft fabric, you will need to apply a special stiffening spray.

The top of a roller blind can not be decorated because the fabric will be wound round it when the blind is closed, but you could fix a pelmet or drape in front of the blind to give it a more finished or elaborate look.

The bottom edge of a roller blind need not be plain as it is never curled right up to the top rod. Scalloped, triangular and crenellated edges can be easily added using the same fabric as the blind, a contrasting colour or complementary fabric. Sequins, shells, silk tassels and a whole host of ornamental trims can be added to the point and curves of the trims.

Roller blinds are generally operated by means of a cord fixed in the middle of the bottom rod. The cord can be plain and simple or dressed up with a glass or wooden bead, a silk tassel, or even a padded felt shape.

Gathered blinds

Gathered blinds are simple panels of fabric that hang straight down in front of the window. When the blind is not needed, you can gather it up by hand and tie it to the top bar with two long strips of material or a decorative rope or ribbon. These are the simplest blinds to make and use.

FAR LEFT: The triangular trim on the lower edge of this star-painted voile roller blind has been finished off with single clear perspex drops, which will sparkle in daylight.

ABOVE: Three separate blinds across this wide window enable the person working at the drawing desk to raise and lower them to suit his or her needs as the sun moves during the day.

LEFT: The crenellated lower edge of this dark bathroom blind picks up the geometric theme of the tile border around the top of the wall and the larger tiles around the bath.

Fancy Edge for a Roller Blind

A fancy border or edging can transform a roller blind. For best effect, choose a plain-coloured blind and use a contrasting patterned fabric for the border, adding trims if you wish. Checks, stripes and geometric designs work particularly well.
You will need: *roller blind, coordinating fabric, tape measure, scissors, tailor's chalk or pen, saucer or plate, pins, needle, thread, sewing machine, glue, braid or ribbon, tassel.*

1 Cut a piece of fabric the width of the blind plus 3cm (1¼in), and double the depth of the required border plus 3.5cm (1⅜in). Fold the fabric over double lengthways with the right sides facing. Draw a line with a pen or tailor's chalk 1.5cm (⅝in) in from the right and left hand edges of the fabric. Using a saucer or plate as a template, draw scallops along the fabric, starting from the centre, 1.5cm (⅝in) in from the bottom fold. Pin the two pieces of fabric together and cut the shapes out 1.5cm (⅝in) lower than the drawn lines.

2 Pin, tack and stitch along the drawn shapes and down either side to 2cm (¾in) from the top. Trim excess fabric. Turn right sides out and press. Turn under 2cm (¾in) along the top of the fabric on either side and press. Place the bottom edge of the roller blind fabric inside the top of the scalloped edge and carefully hand stitch in place with small, neat stitches on either side.

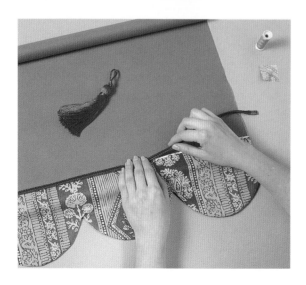

3 Glue and stitch braid or ribbon along the join of the edging and the blind on both sides. Finish the blind with a tassel, bow or rosette (made by gathering a strip of ribbon or braid along one side), securing it with a few stitches.

Contemporary Options

Slat, Venetian or louvred blinds are made up of many narrow strips stacked together one on top of another. The blind can be raised or lowered by means of cords threaded from top to bottom through the slats and the direction in which the slats lie can be adjusted from flat to fully tilted so that they overlap and form a solid blind. Venetian blinds may be made from wood, metal, bamboo or perspex.

Slats made from flexible materials such as thin strips of metal can be easily parted and bowed to allow you to reach your hand through to open the window. Rigid wood and heavy perspex louvres are more difficult to reach through, so you may need to roll up the blind before you can open the window.

Cleaning slat blinds can be time consuming, and with metal varieties, static can build up and attract dust particles. Most established blind companies sell specially made blind cleaners, which you run along the length of each slat; alternatively try using a clean duster on the tip of your finger, or a soft bottle brush.

Vertical blinds, which operate on a similar principle and are usually made from stiffened fabric, are often used in large windows because they can be hung for longer stretches than horizontal blinds, which may sag and be unwieldy if too long.

Natural materials such as bamboo and rush are used for making roller-type blinds. Many of these blinds are sold plain, but you can add your own trimmings and embellishments, such as appliqué fabric designs – leaves and tropical flowers, perhaps – which you can cut out and glue onto the visible surface. Bamboo or rush blinds are best cleaned with a moist sponge of warm, mildly soapy water and left to dry naturally.

Paper blinds are usually made by folding a large piece of paper over and over to create hundreds of tiny pleats. Because the basic material is relatively cheap, paper blinds tend to be inexpensive. They also come in a wide range of colours. The paper is sturdy and holds the folded pleats sharply, and if plain, it can easily be decorated with hand-drawn designs or painted with a stencil. Unusual papers, such as ones from China and Thailand, may be streaked with silk fibres or handmade with pressed flower petals.

LEFT: A pleated paper blind is an inexpensive window dressing and one which you can buy plain and decorate yourself. Because it is lightweight, it is easy to move and hang.
RIGHT: This louvre blind can be raised and lowered to reveal or cover the window. The slats can also be adjusted to lie one on top of the other for a total black out, or horizontally for more light.

Bead Blind

Although it won't provide privacy on its own, this original blind will create a point of interest in a bathroom with an opaque glass window. You could, of course, use coloured beads and string for a very different look.

You will need: doweling, saw, card, ruler, pencil, scissors, cord or string, masking tape, selection of beads and shells, blutack, brass hooks and eyelets, drill and protective goggles (if shells or stones need holes drilling in them).

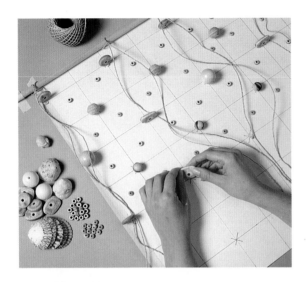

1 Cut a piece of doweling long enough to fit across the window frame. On a piece of card the size of the required blind, draw a grid of 12cm (4¼in) squares. Cut enough lengths of cord, each double the height of the required blind plus an extra 25cm (10in), to go from one end of the doweling to the other at approximately 12 cm (4¼in) intervals. Tape the grid onto a large, flat surface. Attach the cord onto the doweling by folding the cord over double, passing the loop under the doweling and threading the ends of the cord through. Tape the doweling in position across the top of the paper grid.

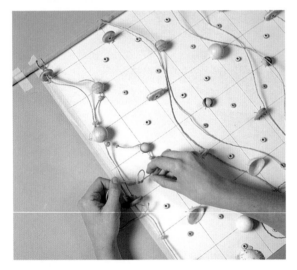

2 Arrange the beads in lines and stick them onto the grid with blu-tack at alternate intersections. Take the first length of cord and thread it through the beads along the vertical edge. If using smaller beads between the large beads, thread these onto the cord and tie a knot underneath. Take the second cord, thread it through the first bead and pull it across and thread through the first bead diagonally to the right (having threaded on a small bead and secured with a knot, if using), then thread through the next bead diagonally to the left. Continue all the way down.

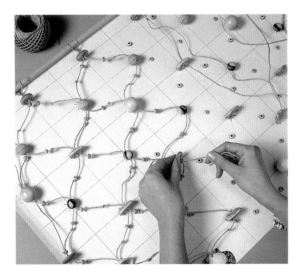

3 Continue across the grid, threading cords in a zig-zag pattern from top to bottom. When all the cords have been threaded, add a final row using shells at the bottom. (If necessary, drill holes in the shells at the top.) Tie the cords with knots at the back of the shells Screw hooks onto the window frame and sit the ends of the doweling in them. Screw eyelets into the bottom of the window frame, pull the outer cord on each side of the blind down, thread through the eyelets and secure with a knot. Twist the eyelets to pull the blind taught. Carefully adjust beads and shells to make straight lines.

Simple Drapes and Screens

Window treatments do not need to be labour intensive and expensive to be effective, some don't even require the use of a sewing machine. A length of sari silk can be draped around a curtain pole or held in place by a few thumb tacks to create a softly draping pelmet, or a sheet of paper can be folded and a lacy border design cut out of it with a sharp pair of scissors, for example. Both are attractive window dressings that take very little time to put together.

Fake curtains

Certain windows may not need to be covered by curtains or blinds because the view is good and the room is not overlooked. In cases like this, where a conventional curtain is not needed, you may possibly still want to create some sort of decoration around the window either to complement the rest of the scheme in the room or to soften the angular frame of the window.

The answer to the problem is the 'permanently' open or fake curtain simply made by draping a length of fabric at the outer edges of the window. This type of dressing can be made from a fraction of the material needed for a formal curtain and seldom requires sewing, apart from hems and edges.

As well as sari silk, mentioned earlier, which comes in a rainbow of wonderful colours, in plain styles or with embroidery, there are many other fabrics and existing sewn cloths you could use. For example, a tablecloth or

bedspread is already hemmed and finished and can easily be adapted as a curtain. These 'faux' window dressings are also useful if you have an antique or old piece of fabric that is not big enough to make a proper curtain or is so precious that you do not want to cut and sew it. They are also ideal, of course, if you want to create an instant and temporary window dressing – for example, if you are not planing on spending long in a house and don't want to buy, cut or sew large lengths of fabric for curtains that many not fit the windows in your new home.

Simple drapes are easy to create with a long, narrow length of material draped either around a pole or between two bosses (one placed at either corner at the top of the window frame). There are a number of looks that can be created in this way. The material can be draped across a pole to form a pelmet and then left to hang down each side to create mock curtains. If the length of fabric you have is shorter, you could be use it to form a simple draped pelmet with two short tails hanging down at either side, or allow it to hang down on one side only – a pelmet with a single long hanging tail.

LEFT: This window has a pleasant view and is not overlooked, so it is an ideal place for a 'pretend' window dressing. A single, long piece of material has been used to create a mock pelmet and two permanently open 'curtains'.
TOP RIGHT: An old piece of material has been used to create a soft pelmet and short 'faux' curtains. The fabric may have been part of an original Victorian dressing for a different size of window, but it can be used again in this informal way, and does not need to be cut or damaged to make it fit the window.
RIGHT: Two contrasting colours of sari silk have been draped around a curtain pole to form an uneven dressing, which adds a soft and decorative surround to a recessed window.

Alternatively, you can simply fold the material in two and pin or staple the centre point to the centre of the window frame, arranging the remainder of the material to form matching drapes or tails on either side of the window frame.

If you use pins or staples to hold the material in place, make sure that you use enough to prevent the fabric from dragging against the pins, as this may damage it. Fine picture tacks are also useful, but these need to be hammered in, so check that the wood of the window frame is in good condition and that the small marks left by the tacks or pins will not be a problem.

The draped style of window decoration is also easy to remove and clean, as there are no hooks or fittings to be dismantled. Drapes can be re-arranged to create different effects, or swapped from room to room when you feel like a change.

No-sew headings

There are more ways of hanging fabric that do away with the need to sew hooks or ruffle tape onto the headings of curtains. Curtain rings with pincer grip clips are ideal for hanging lightweight materials. Spread the curtain rings along the curtain pole at equal distances and then clip the edges of the material to the two end clips. Find the centre point of the fabric and attach it to the centre clip on the pole, then halve each half section and clip that to the pole. Continue to divide each section in two and clip, until all the clips are used. If you don't like the finished effect, you can always unclip it and try again.

Clothes pegs can be used in the same way. Either buy bright plastic pegs, which can look fun in a bathroom, utility room or playroom, or find traditional wooden pegs and paint them to coordinate with the colours in the material you want to hang.

A length of material can be simply folded in two and draped over a rod or pole. If the material is lightweight or has a shiny surface it may be prone to slipping; to prevent this you could put weights in the hems or cover the pole with felt or some other non-slip fabric. Heavy-weight fabrics such as velvet or a rich tapestry will have enough bulk and weight to stay in place if evenly distributed on either side of the pole.

Paper screens

For smaller windows, paper can be used to make simple screens and curtains. The advantage of paper window screens is that they are cheap and easy to make and can be changed frequently. For the very simplest of curtains, fold a sheet of plain white paper in two and drape it over a pole. Decorate the bottom edge by cutting a pattern with a sharp pair of scissors, or use a hole punch to create small holes – a pattern made from repeated punch holes can look like lace.

A sheet of tissue paper or a fine sheet of decorative wrapping paper can be cut to fit the window exactly and held in place with brass drawing pins. Or you could turn the top of the paper back on itself and glue it down to create a channel through which to thread curtain wire or a pole, then attach it to fittings in the window frame.

LEFT: There is no need for ruffle tape and hooks when you use curtain rings with clips, which operate like mini clothes pegs. If you don't like your first arrangement, you can easily release the fabric from the clips and try again.

TOP RIGHT: This window screen has been made to lie flat against the window and take up a mini-mal amount of space. The fabric is held in place by evenly spaced clothes pegs and a wire. Instead of using fabric you could try a sheet of decorative wrapping or tissue paper, cut to fit the window.

RIGHT : For a lower window screen, a half curtain has been made from folded paper decorated with a cut pattern. This cheap and easy curtain can be replaced, rather than washed, when it gets worn.

Second-hand Curtains

It takes many years of use to wear out curtains – they may get a little faded by direct sunlight but they rarely get to be threadbare in less than twenty years, unless given a lot of rough treatment.

There are many ways to come by second-hand curtains. You may move house and bring your curtains

with you, hoping that although they were made for the windows in your old home, they can be adapted to fit in your new one. Someone in your family or a friend may pass on their perfectly good curtains because they've decorated and the old curtains no longer go with the colour scheme, or you may find some wonderful curtains at a sale or auction. In each of these cases the curtains you have may be in good condition but just the wrong size for the windows in your home.

If curtains are too long, it is not a problem, as you can always cut them down to size and re-hem them, but if they are too short or too narrow, what do you do? A generous hem can be let down to give a little additional length, and you can squeeze the very last centimetre out of the fabric if you re-hem using bias binding.

Borders and trims

The simplest way to enlarge curtains by more than a few centimetres is to add a border to them, but the border should be of a good size so that it looks as though it is meant to be there – a small, half-hearted effort will just emphasise the fact that the curtains were too short.

If the curtains are considerably shorter than the window, divide the border in half and sew it to both the top and the bottom of the curtain to give it a more balanced appearance. If the curtain is too narrow as well as too short, you could use the same fabric for all borders – top, bottom and sides (see pages 92-93).

Second-hand curtains may be so small that they can be used as a panel. Take the lining off the old curtain, launder and press, then sew on the borders to bring it up to size. Line the whole piece in one go, and if adding interlining, do that at the same time.

With plain second-hand curtains, you can add a plain

LEFT: These pink and blue check curtains for a child's bedroom have been extended by using a contrasting material in the same pattern. The hard wood pelmet has been painted to complement the colour scheme.
RIGHT: These curtains have been given extra length by dropping the pole down from the top of the window frame. The fish motif, which has been repeated on the quilt, has given a new lease of life to the plain fabric. Stencils and appliqué are a also useful ways to disguise or cover marks.

contrasting border or a patterned one that features the plain colour. With a patterned curtain, a plain border is a clear option, but you could also add another pattern so long as you avoid a dizzying mix of busy designs. To make an extended curtain seem part of the scheme, you could cover or create a pelmet from the border material or add a roller blind in the same colour.

If a curtain is the right length but too narrow, cut it lengthways into two or four and extend it by sewing strips of a contrasting fabric in between the small sections, creating a striped effect. This is particularly effective with plain fabrics of strong, contrasting colours.

Adjusting the heading

Changing the heading of the curtain may also give you valuable extra length. If the curtains have a ruffle or tape heading, remove it and clean and press the curtain so that the heading is flat and unpleated. For the maximum length, use tab or loop tops, which can be made from a contrasting colour of similar weight material. Using curtain rings and hooks will also enable you to hang your curtains a few inches lower than if you use a ruffle tape and conventional track.

A large draped pelmet may also give you a few centimetres leeway at the top of the window if you only need a little extra space to make the curtain reach, as the pelmet can disguise the top of the lowered curtain.

If the curtains are much too short and the window does not need to be covered from top to bottom of the frame, a simple solution is to lower the hanging pole or rod further down the frame (preferably between one third and half way down the frame) until the curtains reach the sill or just below.

Revitalising worn fabrics

Second-hand voiles and fine cotton curtains can be given a new lease of life by washing with a prescribed amount of bleaching agent (if white) or by dying them, either to

'lift' the existing colour or to change them to a different shade. Do remember when dying to a different shade to take the original colour of the curtain into consideration. For example, if the curtain is a dark colour, it will be difficult to make it paler and if the curtain is yellow and you want it to be red, you may have to dye a second time to get the right shade.

Scorch marks or indelible stains can be disguised with appliquéd motifs or bold stencilled designs.

TOP LEFT : This curtain has been extended not only by adding borders at the top, bottom and sides but also by adding strips of the border fabric in the centre of the curtain.

LEFT: Extra width has been created by draping a contrasting shawl over the curtain pole. When the curtains are drawn the shawl can be adjusted to fill any gap between the two curtains.

ABOVE: Tie tops and a 'fake' integral pelmet has given these curtains extra length and the blind using the same check fabric complements them.

Extending Small Curtains

By carefully choosing material that contrasts or co-ordinates with your existing small curtains you can extend them and make a feature of the added border as well as changing the look of the window dressing. Try to choose fabric of a similar weight.
You will need: *old curtains, coordinating fabric, tape measure, scissors, pins, needle, thread, lining, sewing machine, curtain tape, curtain hooks, rings, pole.*

1 Unpick all the hems of the old curtains, remove heading tape and press curtains flat. If original hem marks show, trim away the fabric.. Fold all edges of the old curtain over 3cm (1¼in) for the seam allowance. Measure the width required for the coordinating border all the way round and add 4.5cm (1¾in) for side seam allowances. For top and bottom borders, add 14.5cm (5¾in) for overlapping the corners to make mitres. Lay the strips at right angles to each other and, matching up any pattern or check, mitre the corners to meet at 45 degree angles. Pin, tack and stitch from the outside corner to 1.5cm (½in) in from the inside corner with right sides together. Press the seams open.

2 With right sides together, pin, tack and stitch the border to the old curtain using a 3cm (1¼in) seam allowance. Trim away any excess fabric and press all the seams open.

3 Fold over 3.5cm (1⅜in) along each side of the curtain for the outer hem and press. Cut a piece of lining fabric 3cm (1¼in) smaller than the width of the curtain. With right sides together, pin, tack and stitch the lining in place on either side and at the bottom. Press the seams open. Turn the curtain the right way out and press. Turn the top of the curtain over 10cm (4in) and fold under the raw edge 4cm (1½in). Pin and tack in position. Pin, tack and stitch a length of heading tape across the top of the curtain 2cm (¾in) in from the top of the curtain. Gather the heading tape up by pulling the strings and secure with a knot at each end.

Internal Shutters

Shutters became popular in Georgian times when windows increased in size. They not only offered protection and security, but were also a way of cutting down draughts caused by badly fitting frames and panes. The traditional shutters of this period are panelled and hinged so that they can be folded back into recesses on either side of the window. They were invariably painted the same colour as the walls so that they would blend into the surrounds when not needed.

Now that, in many countries, original panelled shutters are such a feature in a room, you are more likely to find that the panels have been painted in contrasting colours or highlighted by using a darker colour to pick out the bead work around each panel. The more daring might also use the panels as frames by sticking wallpaper or pictures into the centre.

Simple rustic shutters tend not to be panelled but are more likely to be made from tongue-and-groove planks of wood, which slot into each other side by side, or from a single piece of wood. In North America, a number of religious communities, including the Shakers and the Amish, favour shutters above curtains. The Amish, who refrain from embellishment both in dress and in their home, find the shutters practical for their purpose and unobtrusive in design.

Shutters are also popular in Europe and Scandinavia. In southern Europe shutters are used to keep the heat and insects at bay and will often be kept closed in the middle of the day, during siesta, when they are also very effective at shutting out the light. In cooler climes, shutters keep in the warmth.

American-style shutters with adjustable wooden louvres are also popular, and can be made in various sizes so that the top half can be folded away while leaving the bottom of the window shielded by a lower set of shades.

Because shutters fold back on themselves or can be opened out like a window, they offer the same flexibility as traditional curtains. For a recessed window, a small wooden frame with a fabric covering can make a simple, attractive window dressing. The fabric covering will also require less fabric than a traditional curtain. (See page 96 for how to make a simple fabric shutter.)

As an alternative to covering the wooden shutter frame with fabric, why not try using rows of colourful plastic or wooden beads, bottle caps or buttons, threaded onto lengths of cord and knotted to keep them in place, then attached to the top and bottom of the frame.

TOP LEFT: Louvered American-style shutters are used in conjunction with curtains in a traditional living room setting. These full-length shutters are slightly open to allow in a limited amount of light.

LEFT: Two sets of shutters have been used to fill the windows in this modern setting. Not only can the louvres be adjusted to control the flow of light, but the panels can be folded back. Top shutters can be opened to let in light, while the lower ones stay shut to preserve privacy.

ABOVE: Panelled shutters used to be painted the same colour as the wall so as not to be noticed when folded back. These days shutters are usually considered a special feature in a room and are often painted in a contrasting colour.

Fabric Shutters

These simple shutters can be folded back against the wall when not needed, but provide a neat and flat covering for a small window when closed. For a very narrow window, use a single shutter.

You will need: lengths of 12.5mm (½in) wooden strip, ruler, pencil, saw, sandpaper, wood glue, clamps, fabric, scissors, pins, needle, thread, sewing machine, hinges, screws.

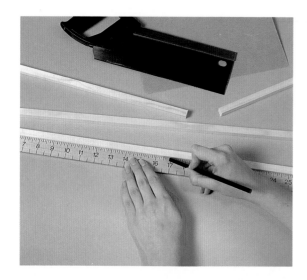

1 Measure the window frame. Cut 4 pieces of wooden strip to fit the height of the frame and 4 pieces to fit half the width of the frame, less 25 mm (1in) allowance for the overlap of the wood at the corners. Sand the ends of the strips until smooth. Lay one long piece of wood on a flat surface and glue and clamp the top and bottom pieces to each end to form a U-shape. Ensure that the corners are all 90 degree angles. Repeat for the second shutter. Leave to dry thoroughly.

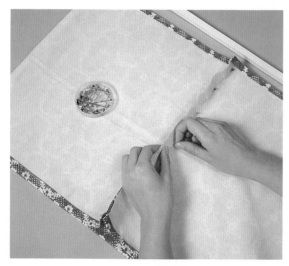

2 Cut two pieces of fabric the width of the inside of the shutters plus 3cm (1¼in) for seam allowance, and twice the length of the shutters plus 8cm (3¼in) for seam allowance. Turn in the seam allowances, then pin, tack and stitch along the outer edges and press. With the right sides facing, fold the fabric around the outside of the shutter frame. Pin and tack the two raw edges together. Remove from the frame and stitch with a machine.

3 Turn the fabric the right way round and again place over the shutter frame. Pin and tack approximately 4cm (1½in) from the top and bottom of the shutters. Remove from the frame and stitch. Pin, tack and stitch the two pieces of fabric together along the sides. Press. Slide onto the frame and glue the second long baton in place. When completely dry, screw the hinges onto the back of the frame and then screw into the window.

Pelmets

A pelmet is a valance or border that hangs over the top of a window and disguises the curtain pole and curtain top. As well as having a practical function, a pelmet is also decorative and can be draped, braided and fringed. Not all windows need pelmets, but if you are following an historical or period style of dressing, such as Georgian or Victorian, then you may find that a pelmet is an appropriate finish for your curtain.

Tall windows often benefit from pelmets, as the pelmet 'caps' the top of the frame and gives a definite end to the top of the curtain; it also helps to lower the overall height of the window. Smaller windows generally require lighter, less ornate pelmets – perhaps nothing more than a simple drape of a light voile or a fine border of lace. Small windows that don't have curtains or blinds can be given a touch of dressing with just a simple pelmet. As a general rule, small recessed windows are best left without a pelmet, as this additional dressing will cut down on the already limited available light.

Pelmets may be hard, softly draped, or formal and padded. Various styles can also be used in combination; for example, a hard pelmet may be placed over a layer of pleated voile or organdie, creating a two-tiered effect.

The pelmet should never dominate the window dressing, but should be an integral part of the overall scheme. If the rest of the furnishings in the room are simple, then opt for a chic and stylish pelmet. If, on the other hand, the colours in your room are rich and the fabrics heavy, you can afford to adopt a more opulent style.

Hard pelmets

Hard pelmets can be made from a thin wood such as plywood or a stiffened hardboard. It is easier to create intricate shapes with a hard pelmet because you can draw and cut the wood accurately and the shape will

hold. They can also be shaped to frame the whole of the window, right down to the sill and even beyond. Hard pelmets can be simply painted or covered in a material that matches or contrasts with the main curtain material. Unusual dressings, such as fine woven raffia or hessian, can also be used. Simply cut the material to size and glue it, using a strong adhesive, to the cut pelmet.

If you are putting a hard pelmet over generously pleated curtains, make sure you allow for the thickness of the curtain when it is pulled back. As this type of pelmet is rigid there will be no give or movement to make extra space for the curtain.

FAR LEFT TOP: This triple-layer pelmet is made up of a plain triangular layer, each point finished with a tassel. Above that a soft pleated layer, and finally a scalloped hardboard pelmet.
FAR LEFT: Unusual fabrics such as woven raffia can be cut to shape and glued to a plywood pelmet. This deep pelmet has been decorated and is used over an Austrian blind, which, when furled up, looks like another decorative pelmet.
ABOVE LEFT: A floor-length pelmet, made from hardboard, frames the whole window and matches the shape and fabric of the chair.
ABOVE: An interesting feature has been cut into the centre of this otherwise traditional pelmet, which has been covered to match the curtains.

Soft draped pelmets

Soft pelmets are often described as swags and tails – the swag being the draped centre part that goes across the width of the window and the tails being the two folded ends that hang down on either side.

These drapes can be styled in many ways, in the same material as the curtain, or in a contrasting colour. The tails can also be lined in another fabric, which shows each time the curtain is furled or pleated. (For more ideas for simple drapes – with or without other curtains – see pages 84-85.)

The soft pelmet can be formal and padded, which gives extra bulk and adds to its grandeur, or it can be as simple as a length of fine silk, simply pleated and arranged around a pole. Between these extremes, there are hundreds of variations to choose from.

The simplest draped pelmet in a light fabric can be created without any backing, but may need a few judicious stitches to keep the folds and pleats in place. Ornate dressings will need to be built up on a backing, such as a sturdy hessian or pliable plastic strip. Some backing materials are made with a peel-off cover, which reveals a sticky surface onto which a layer of material can be smoothed.

The draped material is then arranged over the covered base and carefully stitched in place. Formal drapes, especially if there is another matching pelmet, must be carefully planned so that the distribution of the material is equal and exactly the same on each of the pelmets. The art of creating a successful draped pelmet is to ensure that the drapes look as though they have fallen naturally in place; they should not look too fixed or rigid.

As well as the decoration created by the curls and folds of material, you can add touches such as fringing, braid, bows and rosettes. You could even add tassels, suspending them from the centre of a scoop of fabric. Because of

the amount of fabric and trimmings used, ornate draped pelmets tend to be heavy, so it is important that they are well, and safely, secured to the wall and window frame.

When designing and fixing a pelmet it is worth bearing in mind whether or not you will need to take it down again at any time. Pelmets, like any furnishings in a room, will gather dust, especially if the design incorporates furls and pleats, which create pockets and ledges. A light brush with a feather duster or a gentle vacuum with a hand-held cordless appliance may be enough to dislodge the offending dust deposits, but, if more rigorous cleaning is required, you may need to take the pelmet down.

Velcro provides a practical means of attaching a pelmet to a wooden backing without the need to prise out tacks and nails. Press-stud fasteners, or hooks and eyes are other options that should be suitable for attaching a lightweight pelmet.

LEFT: A fun idea for a child's room, this harlequin-style pelmet has been made from triangles of different coloured material, padded and sewn together in a line. Each point has been finished with a tiny brass bell.

ABOVE: Contrasting material has been used to create a pelmet over these curtains, but instead of the pelmet being hung separately from a pole or board above, it has been sewn onto the top of the curtain.

RIGHT: This formal and very elegant draped pelmet has a central swag and two smaller ones to each side. The tails are neatly and regularly pleated to form a stepped cascade at each side.

Decorated Wooden Pelmet

An extended style of frame like this creates a focal point at the window. This jolly design is perfect for a child's room.
You will need: 7mm (¼in) and 9mm (⅓in) thick medium-density fibreboard (MDF), jig saw, paper, scissors, ruler, pen, sandpaper and wooden block, wood glue, panel pins, hammer, pencil, card, water-based undercoat paint, water-based paints, paint brushes, polyurethane matt varnish, brackets and screws.

1 Measure the window and cut a piece of paper the width of the window plus 4cm (1½in). Fold the paper exactly in half, left to right lengthways, and draw half of the design for the pelmet onto it, drawing any straight lines with a ruler. Cut the shape out. Place the template onto 7mm (¼in) thick medium-density fibreboard (MDF) and secure the corners with masking tape. Draw around the template. Remove the template and cut the shape out with a jig saw. (A mask should be worn when cutting MDF.) Sand smooth the cut edges.

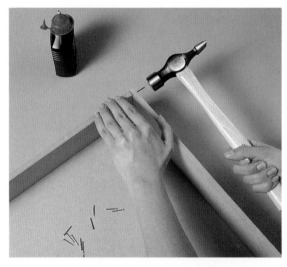

2 Cut 2 lengths of 9mm (⅓in) thick MDF the height of the sides of the pelmet and 8cm (3¼in) wide. Cut another piece for the top, the width of the pelmet less 18mm (ie two thicknesses of MDF) and 8cm (3¼in) wide. Glue the pieces onto the front of the pelmet and secure with panel pins along the side joins and all around the sides and top from the front of the pelmet. Paint with undercoat and leave to dry.

3 Paint the pelmet with the main colour – it may need two coats. Draw a plan of the pelmet decoration onto a piece of paper. Cut a triangle and a flower shape from a piece of card. Place the triangle at the top of the pelmet, starting from the middle, and draw around it with a pencil. Continue all the way along. Draw on the flower shapes using the flower template. Paint the shapes different colours, then add spots randomly all over the pelmet. When dry, paint with varnish. Attach the pelmet to the wall with brackets.

Tie-backs, Tassels and Braids

These finishing touches to a curtain treatment are important as they will give the whole appearance of the window a professional and thoroughly finished look They will also affect how the curtains hang and can provide a useful way of tying in the window dressings with other furnishing fabrics you have used in the room.

Tie-backs and bosses are useful for the practical purpose of keeping curtains away from the edge of the window where they may restrict the amount of light coming into the room and be bleached or damaged by the direct rays of the sun. As well as serving a practical function, tie-backs and bosses can also be an attractive finishing feature for a window dressing.

The curtain can be arranged to adorn the window frame in a sculptural arc which disguises its angular shape. The drape of the curtain can also be used to emphasise the swathe of a decorative pelmet above.

Bosses and curtain hooks

For a simple traditional room, or contemporary scheme, simple wrought-iron or wooden bosses are often the most suitable option. Wrought-iron designs are made in an uneven U shape. The shorter side is attached to the wall and the curtain is simply slipped in behind the longer leg of the hook.

Wooden bosses tend to be a disc or carved shaped, such as a knob or acorn, on the end of a wooden peg. One end of the peg is fixed to the wall and the curtain is draped to the far side of the boss.

Tassels and fabric tie-backs

Silky tassel tie-backs may be chosen to complement the colour of the curtain or as a contrast, and can also highlight any additional trim, such as braid or fringing, that has been added to the curtain. These types of trimmings are suitable for traditional or Victorian schemes. The

Victorian style, which favoured material excess, often had braids and fringe trims with additional tassels at the scoop of each ruche in the pelmet. However, unless you are following an authentic Victorian scheme, it may be best to keep to a more simple arrangement.

Not all tassels are made from the traditional silky yarns, there are many contemporary styles made from natural linen yarn, hessian and jute, sometimes dyed. Tassels come in a range of sizes so choose a tassel that is in proportion to the size and scale, as well as the style, of your window and dressing.

FAR LEFT: A simple wooden disc on a curtain boss has been decorated with an eye-catching geometric design and painted in colours that complement both the wall and curtain material

LEFT: Wrought-iron hooks make an attractive alternative to conventional tie-backs and can be chosen to match curtain poles. Plain fabrics look especially good with this type of hook, as they won't detract from the details of the iron design.

ABOVE: The pelmet and tie-back of a plain curtain are given a dramatic boost by the addition of a contrasting trim. Rich, deep-coloured fringing has been sewn along the lower edge of the tie-back and the edges of the pelmet's swag.

In a children's bedroom or playroom, you might like to make more 'fun' tie-backs, created, for example, from wool pom-poms or from felt shapes sewn together and stuffed, linked by a length of plaited ribbon or wool.

Simple hand-tied bows can also be used to create a curtain tie-back. If you have a plain voile curtain it can be made to taper into a narrow column shape by tying a silk scarf or bow around its middle. If you have more than one curtain, the process can be repeated to create three columns, as seen above, which in turn will allow more daylight into the room.

Traditional fabric-covered tie-backs – crescent shapes of stiffened fabric, usually covered in the same material as the curtain – are a discreet way of holding curtains away from the window. This type of tie-back must be made with a good firm stiffening, or with time and wear it will become wrinkled, saggy and unattractive.

Braids and fringing

Braids and fringing can be used to make elaborate window dressings even more ornate, or to add interest to a simple arrangement. Braids come in a variety of thicknesses and lengths and can be plain, in any number of shades, or multi-coloured. Remember: if your scheme is already busy, it is best to choose the simple, plain-coloured types.

It is important to select special furnishing braids rather than dressmaking types, as they will be larger and more suited to the task. Plain braids can be added to almost any edge of the curtain, from the sides to the hem, but decorative braids and fringing are best shown off on the closing edge of the curtain and on the pelmet.

A contrasting edging can also be made from strips of fabric sewn to make a continuous length, then pinned and sewn along the vertical edge of the curtain and along the edge of a pelmet. Wide ribbons and even bias binding can be used to trim lightweight voile curtains and blinds.

For a dramatic border effect, several rows of braids, sewn side by side, could be used to trim the edge of a curtain, creating a picture frame effect.

Flat trims, such as a sturdy braid or edging of contrasting fabric, not only look attractive, but also offer a certain amount of protection to a curtain edge, which may become worn from regular handling if the curtains are drawn manually. Fringing, if used in a similar way, would be more susceptible to damage and so is better used on curtains drawn by a cord or pole.

LEFT: Three voile curtains are separated by soft, hand-tied bows using contrasting plain-coloured silk scarves. This arrangement allows light to shine through at the bottom.
TOP RIGHT: An ornate dual-coloured silk tassel tie-back is used to secure this curtain away from the window frame.
RIGHT: Tassels come in all shapes, colours and sizes. Traditional tassels are made from silk threads and may be very ornate, but contemporary ones are often much more simple and come in a variety of materials, including natural jute and linen, which is coarser than silk, but none the less attractive.

Windows are a two-way attraction. Not only can they be dressed to add to the interior decoration of a room, as shown in chapter two, but their style and appearance can enhance the exterior of the building too.

The shape and style of window is often dictated by the design of the building in which it sits, but individual decoration, from the drape of the curtain to the colour of paint used on the frame, can make a statement. Adding shutters, window boxes or just fresh bright paint to the frames, sills and surrounds can help to lift an otherwise dull or plain exterior.

Looking In

For example, the lining of a curtain, which can be seen from outside, could be of a bright colour, replacing the more traditional cream or white coloured cotton. Instead of pulling the curtains right back to the edges of the window frame, they can be draped so that they show through the glass of the window.

As well as the fabric adornment, there are many other ways to customise your windows. In this chapter we look at the external decoration of windows, from shutters and window boxes to awnings and balconies, with suggestions for seasonal planting for window boxes that will give you colour and interest on your sill all year round.

Sills and Surrounds

As well as being an important part of the structure of a building, window sills and surrounds can be an attractive feature. Sills and surrounds may be made of wood, stone or metal and painted in contrasting colours or left in their natural state.

The sill is a shelf or slab on which the window sits, and as the window is usually recessed from the outside, the sill normally protrudes a little way beyond the front of the wall of the house. The sill often slopes down and

away from the window, encouraging rain water to run off rather than accumulate and seep through the frame.

Surrounds are the outer frame into which the window is set. Because the window is generally set under the lintel at the top of the surround, it is given a certain amount of protection from rain and wind.

An edging of red bricks in a buff brick wall may be used to create an ornamental surround, or a carved stone lintel above the window may be echoed in plain but matching stone blocks at the sides. Carved lintels, such as those found in older houses, often feature lion's heads or coats of arms. In ancient castles, gargoyles – grotesque carved stone demons – were used as water spouts to carry water clear of the walls, so protecting the façade of the building and the window openings in the way that the window surround has done in more recent times.

On the exterior of a plain brick or stone house, the window frames, sills and door are usually the only places where colour is added. In Ireland, white-washed houses and old thatched cottages often have vivid green or bright blue window surrounds. In some cultures, blue is seen as a colour with religious significance and is frequently used for window frames of whitewashed homes in Mediterranean countries such as Greece.

On timber and clapperboard houses, such as those seen in Scandinavia and New England, frames and surrounds tend to be painted the same colour as the rest of the building, but the windows themselves break up the long expanse of same-coloured wood cladding.

In some countries, sills and surrounds are decorated with more than just paint. On the Channel Island of Guernsey, fishermen traditionally decorated the sills of their houses with pearly centred ormer shells set side by side in the cement of the sill, which glisten in the sun. The shells are also set into the wall under the roof apex.

Maintaining sills and surrounds

Maintenance of window sills and surrounds is important, especially with wooden window frames, where weather damage may cause the timber to rot and decay. Regular repainting is necessary, not only for protection but also for the upkeep of the overall appearance.

It is best to use a specialist masonry or exterior paint for sills and window surrounds as these products are formulated to withstand heat, cold and wet. Ordinary interior emulsion paint will quickly flake and peel if subject to varying weather conditions. Similarly, unpainted wood frames should be treated with a specific weather-resistant stain or preservative, which will protect the wood and increase its waterproof properties.

Most damage to timber frames and sills is caused by wet rot and if the rot reaches the tenons or supports, the whole frame will have to be replaced. Window replacement is an expensive and time-consuming job, which can be avoided by regular stripping and re-painting with a good exterior weather-protective paint.

Sill maintenance is especially important if you have window boxes, as careless and excessive regular watering may cause pools of water to collect below. A good way to protect the sills is to rest the window boxes on terracotta or stone pedestals.

FAR LEFT: This stone surround and sill have been painted in a contrasting colour to the main wall of the house. The interesting crenellated shape is highlighted by the darker colour paint.
TOP LEFT: A plain window sill and surround are painted in a contrasting colour to the pebbledash wall. The row of tiny flowering plants in pots on the window sill give it a more inviting and homely appearance.
LEFT: Regular maintenance of window surrounds and sills is important, especially with wooden frames, where damp may cause rot that will affect the whole window. In Scandinavian countries and parts of North America where weather can be extreme, annual checks are advisable.

Window Boxes

Window boxes bring pleasure to those both inside and outside a building. A flowering window box can bring a breath of the country and a display of nature's bounty even to an inner-city dwelling. From the outside, a colourful window box is an attractive and eye-catching feature.

Window boxes can be made from many types of container. On wide farmhouse sills, old ceramic sinks have been used to create miniature gardens. Painted tin cans filled with sweet scented basil and coriander are often lined up on the sills of Caribbean homes. Individual

terracotta plant pots can be grouped together in an outer box, or an old wrought-iron fire surround can be adapted to make a decorative frame for a wooden box.

Whatever style of window box you choose, do ensure that the pots or box are well secured to the window with brackets or supports. Strong winds may blow pots or boxes off the sill and hurt someone below at ground level, or simply wreck the container and plants.

As mentioned before, window boxes should be kept raised off the sill where possible. Damp that may gather under the box can cause paint to peel and the soil-filled bottom of the box may mark the paint. Two plain bricks can be used as supports for a sturdy terracotta planter or window box, or you could look out for specially made decorative wedges that can be found at good gardening and DIY stores.

As well as being filled with decorative flowers, window boxes can be used to grow herbs and some food stuffs. Miniature tomatoes, such as Tiny Toms, and strawberries can be grown in a deep pot or box, but require regular watering, especially during hot weather. Most herbs – for example parsley, thyme, chives and sage – will grow well in a container, but others, such as rosemary, which grow into larger plants or bushes, will need a big container for satisfactory root growth.

Regular watering is important for window boxes because the limited amount of soil will not retain moisture for long, especially during the summer. If your window box is on a sill that is difficult to reach, you can buy a special capillary watering device, consisting of a plastic bag and a leader tape, which connects the water bag to the window box. The bag will feed water to the box regularly and can be topped up about once a week.

Another device is a pump-action bottle spray, which you should be able to find at a good garden centre. A

two- or three-litre plastic bottle is filled with water and the top screwed on tightly. Using a manual pump, pressure is built up in the container, which raises the water up a long thin rigid pipe that can be directed along the length of the window box.

With good planting and regular feeding and watering, a window box can give pleasure month after month, not only to those who live on the inside, but to those who pass by on the outside as well.

TOP LEFT: Trailing cottage plants and flowers cascade over the sill and cover the bottom of the window frame in a riot of colour.

BELOW LEFT: Foliage can be attractive in its own right. Variegated and interestingly textured leaves such as hostas can create an unusual display. This arrangement is also enhanced by the window bow, which has a decorative panel.

ABOVE: A simple painted wooden window box complements the surround of the window frame and adds to its simple, cottage appearance.

Doweling Window Box

A light and attractive holder for plant pots on the window sill (inside or out). If you are placing the window box outside, do make sure you secure it to the walls or sill so that it won't slip or blow off.

You will need: doweling, ruler, pencil, saw, sandpaper, wood glue, masking tape, sheets of newspaper, wood stain suitable for exterior use, paint brush, twine, scissors, 5 x terracotta plant pots (9cm/3¹/₂in tall).

1 Cut 8 lengths of doweling x 54cm (21¹⁄₄in), 12 lengths x 11cm (4¹⁄₄in) and 8 lengths x10cm (4in). You can increase or decrease the lengths depending on the size and number of pots you are using. Sandpaper the ends of the doweling until smooth. Paint the wood stain evenly onto the doweling and allow to dry.

2 Lay 2 pieces of the long doweling 10 cm (4in) apart and glue 6 pieces of 10 cm (4in) doweling at regular intervals along them, placing the first and last at the very ends of the long pieces. Lay two 10cm (4in) batons 54cm (21¹⁄₄in) apart, and glue the remaining long pieces of wood onto them. Leave to dry. Prop these up 11 cm (4¹⁄₄in) apart, and glue a piece of 11 cm (4¹⁄₄in) doweling to each end, so joining the top and bottom of the box. Secure with masking tape. Glue the other pieces along the side in line with the batons across the top. When dry remove the tape, turn over and repeat along the other side.

3 Cut 24 lengths of twine approximately 30cm (12in) long. Thread a piece of twine under one of the batons, across the top and pull out the other side. Pull both ends down and cross them over each other over the upright baton. Pull both ends round the back and up to the top baton and cross over each other again. Pull down under the baton and secure firmly with a knot under the top baton. Continue on all joints.

Planting Ideas

Window boxes need a good layer of drainage at the bottom – gravel or broken bit of old terracotta plant pot will do. If the container is plastic, punch a few holes in the base to allow excess water to drain away, otherwise the plants may become waterlogged and rot.

On top of the drainage material add a good soil and compost mix – you will find specially formulated composts for window boxes and containers at most good garden centres. Once the box is well filled with compost, plant out your blooms – plants or bulbs – and water well.

When planning a planting scheme, bear in mind the size to which each plant will grow. Place taller plants in the centre and medium-height ones on either side, then use small edging plants to fill in under the taller ones and to the edges of the box. If you wish to add some trailing plants, put them to the outer edges of the box.

Seasonal planting

For a spring show, you may like to plant up a display of bulbs, such as crocus, aconites, hyacinths, miniature irises, tulips and daffodils. (Regular-height varieties may be too tall and ungainly for a small window box.) Plant spring-flowering bulbs in the autumn.

Summer arrangements can include members of the brightly coloured geranium family, especially the trailing varieties that will hang over the edge of the box. Begonias also come in a variety of shades, and marigolds, in orange and yellow, give a real splash of colour. Fuchsias and busy lizzies (*Impatiens*) are useful for the pink and red end of the colour spectrum and grape hyacinths and anemones will add a dash of purple and blue. Smaller plants, such as lobelia, can be used to fill in beneath taller plants and create a box full of flowers.

For autumn and winter planting, polyanthus and pansies, bedding plants such as wall flowers, and leafy creepers, such as ivy, will give a lasting show of colour. You can also plant all-season boxes with dwarf conifers, miniature roses and heathers, but remember, if you plan to keep a single display going for a long time, that these all-season boxes will need regular watering and feeding with a good plant food to replenish the nutrients that the plants take from the soil.

Theme planting

You could also plant to a theme, for example an alpine selection of plants such as saxifrage, alyssum, gentians (which are difficult to grow but a delight if you succeed), campanula and the creeping mountain avens.

A scented selection will fill the room with perfume on hot evenings when the window is left open. Try dianthus or rockery pink, a small carnation-like flower with a sweet smell. Stocks, especially the night-scented variety, and nicotiana, the tobacco plant, have the most seductive perfume, but they may grow tall, so look out for a dwarf hybrid, which will be better suited to a window box. Herbs such as lemon balm and mint give off their scent when their leaves are rubbed.

LEFT: A good mix and combination of colours make this summer window box appealing. Pale and strong colours should alternate and the area under taller plants should be filled in with shorter spreading plants, such as trailing campanula.
ABOVE RIGHT: In this box, a variegated ivy trails over the edge and a young aucuba, gives the centre of the arrangement a focal point and height. These two plants could stay in the box throughout the year and fresh seasonal plants could be added when needed. Pansies are good in summer and winter alike.
RIGHT: You don't have to plant a window box full of flowers – interesting foliage plants, such as the different types of coleus (flame nettle) and silver-leaved cineraria (dusty miller) shown here, can be just as attractive.

Shutters and Awnings

External window dressings, such as shutters and awnings, provide an opportunity to bring colour and interest to the outside of a building and have been popular over the centuries. Modern homes with air conditioning and UV-reductive glass windows may not need them, but they are still attractive accessories.

External shutters

Shutters are probably the earliest form of window covering – certainly they were in use long before the invention of glass. When man first made an opening in a wall, a plank of wood, or several pieces of wood joined together, would have been the simplest way to close the opening over again.

External shutters are very useful as well as attractive. They are a good burglar deterrent as they are difficult to prize open, especially if they are locked from the inside with large metal bars. Shutters also keep out the heat of the midday sun, particularly in Mediterranean countries and the southern States of America.

Shutters are also decorative, especially when painted in attractive colours. In countries such as Switzerland, householders take pride in adding brightly painted symbols and motifs to their shutters. Designs – popularly hearts – can also be cut through the wooden panel, creating a peephole feature.

Wood is the most common material used to make shutters, but they come in a variety of styles. Solid wood shutters made from planks of wood nailed side by side, with little or no embellishment are common in rural areas. These functional, rather than decorative, features obscure the light completely and keep insects at bay.

ABOVE LEFT: This rustic shutter is a practical way of keeping the window secure and blocking out the light. What it lacks in embellishments, it makes up for in simple, quaint charm.
LEFT: Both solid and louvred types of shutter have been combined here to create a window shield that allows a small amount of light and air flow through the top .
RIGHT: Both shutters and awnings have been used at the front of this house for maximum protection as well as strong visual appeal.

Other types of wooden shutters are panelled and hinged to that they can be folded back in sections, allowing variable amounts of light into the room. Louvred shutters have fixed-angle slats so that a little light and air passes through them, but they still provide protection against the glare of the sun.

External shutters fixed to the outside of the window are practical because they can be folded back flat against the wall when daylight is needed in the room. The shutters will also close over any plants and pots on the window sill, keeping them safe from night frost.

Shutters are also made from sheets of metal. These are more usually found covering the windows of commercial properties, but some have found their way into domestic use. Metal shutters may work on the same opening and closing principles as wooden shutters or be constructed to furl up around a central roller and fold neatly away out of sight when not in use.

Awnings and sun blinds

As well as shutters, a popular way of keeping the effects of the hot sun at bay is to install awnings or sun blinds. Awnings were originally made of sturdy canvas and can be traced back to the seventeenth century when they were used on ship's decks to provide shelter for the crew against both sun and rain.

These days awnings are more often made from heavy-duty nylon or plastic, which has a longer life than untreated canvas. Blinds made from canvas will fade due to the bleaching effect of direct sunlight and may also rot if frequently drenched by rain. Canvas is also prone to mildew and mould if put away while damp. Although not as aesthetically pleasing as canvas, the manmade materials such as nylon and plastic do have better colour fastness and durability.

Awnings are often bright and patterned, making them an attractive feature at the front of a building. Stripes, like those seen on old-fashioned deckchairs, are most popular and add to the gaiety of their appearance.

When not in use, an awning can be pushed back over a roller so that it furls into a narrow column, which lies flat against the wall of the house. When it is needed, it is simply pulled down either by hand or with the help of a long pole with a brass hook at the end.

Awnings over balconies act as a shade for those sitting out, as well as protection for the front of the house and the furnishings inside. Like a large garden umbrella, the awning will provide a cool and sheltered area in which to entertain, or just sit and relax.

As awnings and shutters both take the brunt of the weather they need to be regularly and well maintained. Wooden shutters will need to be stripped down and re-varnished or painted to sustain the weatherproof finish and prevent the timber from rotting. Awnings should be left to dry thoroughly before they are rolled away to prevent water damaging the material and rusting the joints and roller mechanism.

LEFT: Louvred shutters like these are often found on Colonial-style buildings and on homes in the southern States of America.

ABOVE TOP: Secure locking mechanisms can be seen on the inside of these wooden tongue-and-groove shutters. When locked closed, these shutters will provide a good defence against burglary.

ABOVE: These shutters open back flat against the wall of the house when not in use, allowing maximum daylight into the room inside. Privacy is provided by interesting 'trompe l'œil' net curtains.

Balconies

Famous as the location of Romeo and Juliet's fabled meeting in Shakespeare's play, the balcony has often been endowed with romantic connotations.

In flats and apartments, where there is no access to a garden, the balcony is the only private area in which to sunbathe or enjoy the air. Balconies often become miniature gardens with flowers, shrubs and even trees planted in pots and other containers. Barbecues, tables, deckchairs and loungers may also make their way out onto the balcony if there is space.

Safety is an important factor for a balcony; strong waist-high railings are essential to prevent people and

plant pots from toppling over the edge. In older buildings, ornate wrought-iron railings often provide a decorative feature as well as a security device.

In European countries such as Italy, Austria, Germany and Switzerland, where people tend to live in flats rather than houses, balconies and window sills are often decorated with troughs of bright flowers. Most popular in the warmer countries are geraniums, which have prolific, long-lasting flowers in vibrant shades of red and pink that withstand the heat of the long summers.

Modern apartment blocks often have communal balconies that act as walkways, giving access to each flat. These are more difficult to decorate, but you could attach narrow boxes to railings and place tubs of shrubs on either side of the front door, provided they don't restrict movement along the passage.

Hanging baskets can also provide an attractive way of displaying flowers without encroaching on the usually limited floor space available on a balcony. Terracotta wall pots and troughs are attractive alternatives to hanging baskets; both usually have a flat back panel and a rounded front and can be attached easily to the wall with a couple of stout screws.

If you have drainpipes running down past your balcony, why not disguise them by growing a climbing plant, such as an ivy or Virginia creeper, from a pot at its base and using the pipe as a support for the plant. Alternatively, attach pots with circular clips onto the drainpipe – if you grow a cascading plant out of the pot, it will create a screen in front of the offending pipe.

On the ground floor a balcony becomes a veranda, also with a railed front. Verandas and balconies are features often found on the front of houses in hot climates, colonial houses in the Caribbean and houses in the southern States of America. Not only are they attractive

FAR LEFT: This communal balcony runs in front of a row of flats giving access to the apartments. By this flat it has a decorative purpose and is hung with small but flower-filled containers which bring colour to the otherwise plain exterior of the building.

ABOVE: Fine wooden railings along the first-floor balcony and ground floor veranda of this house provide safety but also look attractive. This style of balcony and veranda can be found in old Colonial houses, especially in the Carribean.

LEFT: Sturdy stone buttresses support this narrow balcony outside a first-floor window. Decorative wrought-iron railings provide safety, and abundant troughs of flowers add to the appeal of the building both inside and out.

and provide a sheltered area in which to sit out, they also protect the front of the house from extremes of weather and sunlight.

French windows

A French window is really a door, or pair of small doors made up from a wooden frame and several small panes of glass. French windows may also be extended casement windows – in old English houses you have to stoop to step under the upper half of the window and out to the garden or grounds.

Although French windows are found on the ground floor of buildings, they are often also located on the upper floors, where they open out onto balconies or terraces. French windows give an illusion of space as the long tall shape allows more light into the room, and even if they lead out only onto a tiny balcony, they give a feeling of space beyond.

From the outside of a building French windows can be a focal point as they are more unusual in size and shape than a standard window. And if a climbing plant , such as a rose, clematis or wysteria, is trained to grow around them, the plants will create an attractive arch or bower. This sort of planting is also beneficial from the inside – when the windows are opened on a summer's evening the scent of the flowers will waft into the room.

TOP LEFT: Built over an archway, this small balcony provides a vantage point from which the inhabitants of the room behind can enjoy the view and take the air. Bowed iron railings and flowers make it attractive.
LEFT: The railings of this London balcony are disguised by a mass of vegetation; pots of plants, shrubs and trees transform a cement terrace into a private garden with a magnificent view of the River Thames.
RIGHT: French windows are really doors, they can lead from a basement or ground floor room out to a garden or from a first floor room onto a balcony.

Picture Credits

The publishers wish to thank the following photographers, picture libraries, companies and PR agencies who have supplied photographs for this book. All the above and, where appropriate, the title of the magazine in which the picture was first featured, are credited by page number and , where necesary, position on the page: (B) Bottom, (T) Top, (C) Centre, (BL) Bottom Left etc.

Half-title page: Debi Treloar/Homes & Gardens/Robert Harding Syndication

Title page: Sanderson

Title verso: William Mason/Ingrid Mason Pictures

Contents page: Sanderson

Page 6: Christopher Drake/Country Homes & Interiors/ Robert Harding Syndication

Page 7: Paul Bricknell/Ideal Home/Robert Harding Syndication

Page 8: Marie-Louise Avery/Ingrid Mason Pictures

Page 9: Lewis/Edifice

Page 10: Tom Leighton/Homes & Gardens/Robert Harding Syndication

Page 11: Marie-Louise Avery/Ingrid Mason Pictures

Page 12: Marie-Louise Avery/Ingrid Mason Pictures

Page 13: (TL) Lewis/Edifice, (BL) Alex Ramsay, (TR) Lewis/Edifice

Page 14: Lewis/Edifice

Page 15: Alex Ramsay

Page 16: (T) Sue Atkinson, (B) Tom Leighton/Homes &Gardens/ Robert Harding Syndication

Page 17: Alex Ramsay

Page 18: The Velux Company Ltd

Page 19: (T) Homes & Gardens/Robert Harding Syndication, (B) Crowson Fabrics

Page 20: Pilkington Glass Ltd

Page 21: IKEA

Page 22: Homes & Gardens/Robert Harding Syndication (T) Lewis/Edifice, (B) IKEA

Page 24: Sue Atkinson/© Salamander Books Ltd

Page 25: Sue Atkinson/© Salamander Books Ltd

Page 26: Brad Simmons/Robert Harding Picture Library

Page 27: (T) Marie-Louise Avery/Ingrid Mason Pictures, (B) Andreas von Einsiedel

Page 28: Lewis/Edifice

Page 29: Christopher Drake/Woman's Journal/Robert Harding Syndication

Page 30: IKEA

Page 31: (T) The Shutter Shop, (B) Darley/Edifice

Page 32: Alex Ramsay

Page 33: (T) Debi Treloar/Homes & Gardens/Robert Harding Syndication, (B) Lara Grylls PR

Page 34: Sue Atkinson/© Salamander Books Ltd

Page 35: Sue Atkinson/© Salamander Books Ltd

Page 36: Tim Imrie/Ideal Home/Robert Harding Syndication

Page 37: Byron & Byron

Page 38: Artisan

Page 39: Sanderson

Page 40: Sue Atkinson/© Salamander Books Ltd

Page 41: Sue Atkinson/© Salamander Books Ltd

Page 42: Debi Treloar/Homes & Gardens/Robert Harding Syndication

Page 43: Marie-Louise Avery/Ingrid Mason Pictures

Page 44: (T) Jan Baldwin/Country Homes & Interiors/ Robert Harding Syndication, (B) Pret à Vivre

Page 45: Sanderson

Page 46: Pret à Vivre

Page 47: Sue Atkinson/© Salamander Books Ltd

Page 48: Pret à Vivre

Page 49: (L) David Chivers/Homes & Gardens/ Robert Harding Syndication, (R) Marie-Louise Avery/ Ingrid Mason Pictures

Page 50: James Merrell/Country Homes & Interiors/ Robert Harding Syndication

Page 51: Graham Rae/Ideal Home/Robert Harding Syndication

Page 52: Trevor Richards/Homes & Gardens/ Robert Harding Syndication

Page 53: (T) Jan Baldwin/Homes & Gardens/ Robert Harding Syndication, (B) Simon Upton/ Country Homes & Interiors/Robert Harding Syndication

Page 55: Brad Simmons/Robert Harding Picture Library

Page 56: Christopher Drake/Homes & Gardens/ Robert Harding Syndication

Page 57: (T) Graham Rae/Ideal Home/Robert Harding Syndication, (B) Tim Beddon/Homes & Gardens/ Robert Harding Syndication

Page 58: Tim Beddon/Homes & Gardens/Robert Harding Syndication

Page 59: (T) Ideal Home/Robert Harding Syndication, (B) Sanderson

Page 60: Crowson Fabrics

Page 61: Dominic Blackmore/Homes & Ideas/ Robert Harding Syndication

Page 62: Graham Rae/Ideal Home/Robert Harding Syndication

Page 63: (T) Dominic Blackmore/Homes & Ideas/Robert Harding Syndication, (B) Graham Rae/Ideal Home/ Robert Harding Syndication

Page 64: Hill & Knowles

Page 65: Crowson Fabrics

Page 66: Jan Baldwin/Homes & Gardens/Robert Harding Syndication

Page 67: (T) IKEA, (B) Sanderson

Page 68: Sunway blind from Hunter Douglas Window Fashions

Page 69: S. Powell/Ideal Home/Robert Harding Syndication

Page 71: Sunway blind from Hunter Douglas Window Fashions

Page 72: Ideal Home/Robert Harding Syndication

Page 73: (T) Tim Imrie/Country Homes & Interiors/ Robert Harding Syndication, (B) IKEA

Page 74: Sue Atkinson/© Salamander Books Ltd

Page 75: Sue Atkinson/© Salamander Books Ltd

Page 76: Christopher Drake/Homes & Gardens/ Robert Harding Syndication

Page 77: (T) IKEA, (B) Ideal Home/Robert Harding Syndication

Page 78: Sue Atkinson/© Salamander Books Ltd

Page 79: Sue Atkinson/© Salamander Books Ltd

Page 80: Ideal Home/Robert Harding Syndication

Page 81: IKEA

Page 82: Sue Atkinson/© Salamander Books Ltd

Page 83: Sue Atkinson/© Salamander Books Ltd

Page 84: Christopher Drake/Country Homes & Interiors/ Robert Harding Syndication

Page 85: (T) Tim Beddow/Country Homes & Interiors/ Robert Harding Syndication, (B) Di Lewis/Ideal Home/ Robert Harding Syndication

Page 86: Christopher Drake/Homes & Gardens/ Robert Harding Syndication

Page 87: (T) Debi Treloar/Homes & Gardens/ Robert Harding Syndication, (B) Jan Baldwin/ Homes & Gardens/Robert Harding Syndication

Page 88: Dominic Blackmore/Homes & Ideas/ Robert Harding Syndication

Page 89: Tom Leighton/Homes & Gardens/Robert Harding Syndication

Page 90: (T) David Chivers/Robert Harding Syndication, (B) Tom Leighton/Country Homes & Interiors/ Robert Harding Syndication

Page 91: Gavin Kingcome/Homes & Gardens/ Robert Harding Syndication

Page 92: Sue Atkinson/© Salamander Books Ltd

Page 93: Sue Atkinson/© Salamander Books Ltd

Page 94: (T) Firifiss (Lara Grylls PR), (B) House of Shutters

Page 95: Trevor Richards/Homes & Gardens/ Robert Harding Syndication

Page 96: Sue Atkinson/© Salamander Books Ltd

Page 97: Sue Atkinson/© Salamander Books Ltd

Page 98: (T) Christopher Drake/Country Homes & Interiors/ Robert Harding Syndication, (B) Christopher Drake/ Homes & Gardens/Robert Harding Syndication

Page 99: (L) Sanderson, (R) Tim Imrie/Ideal Home/ Robert Harding Syndication

Page 100: Dominic Blackmore/Homes & Gardens/ Robert Harding Syndication

Page 101: (T) Polly Wreford/Homes & Gardens/ Robert Harding Syndication, (B) Crowson Fabrics

Page 102: Sue Atkinson/© Salamander Books Ltd

Page 103: Sue Atkinson/© Salamander Books Ltd

Page 104: (L) James Merrell/Country Homes & Interiors/ Robert Harding Syndication, (R) Artisan

Page 105: Ideal Home/Robert Harding Syndication

Page 106: Di Lewis/Ideal Home/Robert Harding Syndication

Page 107: (T) William Mason/Ingrid Mason Pictures, (B) Sue Atkinson/© Salamander Books Ltd

Page 108: Fritz von der Schulenburg/Country Homes & Interiors/ Robert Harding Syndication

Page 109: William Mason/Ingrid Mason Pictures

Page 110: Alex Ramsay

Page 111: (T) Marie-Louise Avery/Ingrid Mason Pictures, (B) Adam Woolfitt/Robert Harding Picture Library

Page 112: (T) William Mason/Ingrid Mason Pictures, (B) Sue Atkinson

Page 113: Robert Harding Picture Library

Page 114: Sue Atkinson/© Salamander Books Ltd

Page 115: Sue Atkinson/© Salamander Books Ltd

Page 116: Sue Atkinson

Page 117: Sue Atkinson

Page 118: (T) Marie-Louise Avery/Ingrid Mason Pictures, (B) Sue Atkinson

Page 119: Robert Harding Picture Library

Page 120: Homes & Gardens/Robert Harding Syndication

Page 121: Sue Atkinson

Page 122: John Neubauer/The Garden Picture Library

Page 123: (T) Marie-Louise Avery/Ingrid Mason Pictures, (B) William Mason/Ingrid Mason Pictures

Page 124: (T) Marie-Louise Avery/Ingrid Mason Pictures, (B) John Glover/The Garden Picture Library

Page 125: (T) Marie-Louise Avery/Ingrid Mason Pictures

Index

Page numbers in italic refer to illustrations and captions

A

anti-climb paint 30
apex windows *15*
appliqué work 52, 53
arched windows 16, *16*
Arts and Crafts Movement 14, 16
Austrian blinds *69,* 70, 72
awnings 121

B

balconies 122-124, *122-124*
basement rooms 26
bathrooms 17, *17,* 33, 44-45, *44,* 50, 58
bay windows 12, *13,* 14, 33
bead blinds 82, *82-83*
blinds 44-45, *44,* 49, 68-83
   combined with curtains 58-60
   measuring for 70-71, *70*
bosses 104
bow windows 12, *13,* 14, 33
braids 106-107
brocade *46*
bulls-eye glass *13,* 20

C

carpets 46
cascade blinds 70-71, 72, 74, *74-75*
casement windows 12
catches 28, *28-29*
chintz *46*
church windows 16
coloured glass 20
contemporary windows 14
corded cotton *46*
crewelwork 50, *50*
crown glass *13,* 20
curtain hooks 104
curtains
   borders 88-90
   combined with blinds 58-60
   extending 92, *92-93*
   fake 84-87
   finished look 63
   headings 64-67, *64-67,* 90
   heavyweight 50
   hems 67, *67*
   length 56-58
   materials 44-54
   measuring for 54, *54*
   outer 60-63
   period 56
   second-hand 88-93
   treatments 56-63
   trims 88-90

D

diamond-paned windows 12
dormer windows 19, *19*
double glazing 23
drapes 84-87, *84-85*
drill *46*

E

electric sensors 30

F

fabrics see materials
fancy blinds 72-73
fanlights 12
   triangular *16,* 19
festoon blinds 70, 72, *72*
film-applied glass 22
finials *36-39,* 37-38
   clay 40, *40-41*
flat headings 67

F (cont.)

French pleats *65*
French windows 124
fringing 106-107

G

gathered blinds 76
gathered headings 64
Georgian style 12, *13,* 14, 56
glass
   bricks *22*
   coloured 20
   decorative 20
   double glazing 23
   laminated 22
   patterned 20
   reinforced 30
   safety 21-23
   stained 16, 20, 23
   stencilled 24, *24-25*
   types of 20-25
Gothic Revival 16

H

hand-pleated headings 64-66, *64*
   handles 28
   headings 64-67, *64-67*
   adjusting 90
   no-sew 86-87, *86*
hems *67, 67*
hessian 46, *46, 51*

J

jacquard *46*

K

kitchens *21,* 44-45

L

lace 48-49, *48-49*
laminated glass 22
leaded glass *13*
linen *46*
locks 30
louvred blinds 80, *81*
louvred shutters 30, *31,* 94, *95*
lozenge-paned windows 12

M

materials
   choosing 44-54
   revitalizing 52-53, 90-91
   types of 46, *46-47*
   unusual 50-52
moire *46*
muslin *46*

O

organdie 60

P

paper blinds 80, *80*
pelmets 98-100, *98-103*
   decorated 102, *102-103*
   hard 98-99
   soft-draped 100
plants 26, *26*
pocket headings *65,* 66-67
poles 36, *36-37,* 58
port-hole style windows 16-17, *17*

Q

quilting 52

R

radiators 33
raffia *6, 46*

R (cont.)

recessed windows 19, *19, 44*
rectangular windows 16
reinforced glass 30
replacement windows 14
ribbed cotton *46*
roller blinds 44-45, *44,* 49, *68,* 70, *71, 76, 76-77*
   combined with curtains 58-60, *63*
   fancy edge for 78, *78-79*
Roman blinds 71, 76
round windows 14, 16-19, *17*
ruched blinds 72-73

S

safety glass 21-23
sand-blasted glass 14
sari silk *53,* 84
sash windows 12, *13*
   fasteners 28
screens 87, *87*
screw bolts 28, 30
sealed units 23
secondary glazing 23
security 28, 30, *30-31*
security glass 21-23, 30
shelves, window 26, *26, 27*
shutters
   external 118-120, *118-121*
   fabric 96, *96-97*
   internal 12, 30, *31,* 94-95, *94-97*
sills, external 110-111, *110-111*
slat blinds 80
slub silk *46*
stained glass 16, 20, *23*
stencilling
   curtains 52, *52,* 53
   glass 24, *24-25*
   voile 48, *48*
storage, window seats 33
sun blinds 121

T

tassels 104-106
textured glass *20, 21*
tie-backs 38, 58, 104-107, *105-107*
toughened glass 22-23
triangular windows 19
Tudor style 14, 56

U

unusual-shaped windows 16-19
upholstery 46

V

velvet *46*
Venetian blinds 80, *81*
vertical blinds 80
voile *46,* 48-49, *48-49,* 60
   second-hand 90-91

W

window boxes 112-113, 112-117
   doweling 114, *114-115*
   planting 116-117
window catches 28, *28-29*
window seats 32-33, *32, 33*
   cushions 33, *33-34*
window shelves 26, *26, 27*
windows
   period 12
   styles 12-14
wool *46*
wrought-iron screens 30